THE PROPHETS I

The Storyteller's Companion to the Bible ™

Michael E. Williams, editor
VOLUME SIX

THE PROPHETS I

Abingdon Press
Nashville

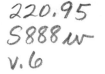
THE PROPHETS I

Library of Congress Cataloging-in-Publication Data

The Storyteller's companion to the Bible.
  Includes indexes.
  Contents: v. 1. Genesis—v. 2. Exodus-Joshua—[etc.]—v. 6. The Prophets.

  1. Bible—Paraphrases, English. 2. Bible—Criticism, interpretation, etc. I. Williams, Michael E. (Michael Edward), 1950-
BS550.2.S764   1991   220.9'505   90-26289
ISBN 0-687-39670-0 (v. 1 : alk. paper)
ISBN 0-687-39671-9 (v. 2 : alk. paper)
ISBN 0-687-39672-7 (v. 3 : alk. paper)
ISBN 0-687-39674-3 (v. 4 : alk. paper)
ISBN 0-687-39675-1 (v. 5 : alk. paper)
ISBN 0-687-00838-7 (v. 6 : alk. paper)
ISBN 0-687-00120-X (v. 7: alk. paper)

01 02 03 04 05 — 10 9 8 7 6 5 4 3 2

To the staff and congregation of
Belle Meade United Methodist
Church, without whose generous encouragement
and support these volumes would not have
been possible.

And, as always for
Margaret
Sarah
and
Elizabeth

(M. E. W.)

Contributors

Mary Donovan Turner holds a Ph.D. from Emory University, where she studied Old Testament and Preaching. She is currently teaching at the Pacific School of Religion and the Graduate Theological Union. She is widely sought after as a preacher and lecturer. As editor of this volume I personally appreciate her determination and persistence as she overcame a brain tumor and significant loss of sight to write these comments.

R. Michael Sanders retold the stories based upon the texts from Isaiah. He is pastor of First United Methodist Church in Grayville, Illinois. He is the author of *The Pastor's Unauthorized Instruction Book* (Abingdon) and has written for various church periodicals including *The Door.*

Edward W. Thorn retold the stories based on Hosea, Amos, Micah, Habakkuk, and Zephaniah. He earned his Ph.D. at Indiana University. He taught for twenty years in the Communications Department of Florida Southern College. Currently, he is pastor of First United Methodist Church of Perry, Florida. He is the author of the forthcoming book *Hoof 'n Mouth Disease: Biblical Monologues and How to Do Them* (Lima, Ohio: C.S.S. Publishing).

Michael E. Williams is one of the pastors at Dalewood United Methodist Church in Nashville, Tennessee. He earned his Ph.D. in oral interpretation from Northwestern University and previously directed the Office of Preaching for The United Methodist Church.

Contents

A Storyteller's Companion

Michael E. Williams

This volume, Prophets I, like the previous five in the Storyteller's Companion to the Bible Series, is written for anyone interested in telling Bible stories. Pastors who encounter readings in the lectionary from the prophetic tradition or who choose to preach on prophetic texts will find this volume particularly helpful as they prepare to put the flesh and blood of a sermon on the skeleton provided by a prophetic utterance. If preaching is to help the listener participate in the world of the Scriptures, then telling stories that make the teachings of the thinkers of our faith tradition come alive is imperative.

In addition, leaders of Bible studies may be called upon to "explain" the meaning of a prophetic saying. What better way to answer a call for explanation than the ways the ancient rabbis and sages did, by telling a story? The first five volumes have been used for personal Bible study by many individuals looking for alternate resources for enriching their knowledge of Scripture. It may also be that parents or grandparents will want to tell stories that flesh out some bit of traditional wisdom as they act as the first, and perhaps most significant, teachers in their families.

We live in what some call the information age, and we truly have more facts about a greater variety of subjects at our fingertips than during any previous time in history. To gather many bits of information without seeing any pattern in which they have meaning for us is a very trivial pursuit, as the name of the game suggests. We might say that to have knowledge rather than just an assortment of facts means that we know the *why* behind the *what*. This is often provided by the system of shared values within a society. The words of the prophets still challenge all our trivial pursuits.

The people hear their prophets who accuse them of unfaithfulness to God. The consequences of such breaking faith is exile. The experience of exile is not limited to the ancient world. In the history of North America, the treatment of Native Americans, especially on the Trail of Tears for the Cherokee people in the early nineteenth century, parallels the experience of the exiles of old.

More recently, all we need to do is look at the morning newspaper or watch the evening news broadcast to view the devastation of a people faced by violence in their homeland. In Bosnia, Rwanda, and Haiti we have seen, in recent times, populations decimated by violence. The survivors run for their very lives, but instead of emigrating to the safety of other countries, these exiles too often find no welcome anywhere.

We have also experienced return and restoration among Palestinians in Gaza and the West Bank. The problems of establishing stable government leadership and a society free from turmoil after years of absence of stability and repression—even terrorism—are as much a part of our modern experience as they were for the people of God to whom the prophets of the exile spoke.

The storyteller must realize that exile can be experienced from many perspectives. How many times have we sent people to "Babylon" in an attempt to destroy their culture or assert that our culture is superior to the native culture? We must hear the cries of the exiles and God's promises to them.

The Stories

While we attempt in this volume to be comprehensive in our approach to pre-exilic prophets, we obviously are not able to include them all. We have included the vast majority of texts that appear in *The Revised Common Lectionary*, 1992 (the most inclusive so far). But, in addition, we have gone far beyond the scope of these lectionaries to include stories that make a significant contribution to the biblical prophetic tradition as a whole.

If you do not find one of your favorite passages of Scripture in this collection, there is no need for you to despair. Much of the information you will learn from the comments on the stories that are included immediately after each story can be transferred to other texts. This will allow you to use your creativity more fully.

The translation from which the printed texts in The Storyteller's Companion are taken is *The Revised English Bible*. You may wish to compare the readings here with your favorite translation or with several other versions. Your familiarity with several translations of the Bible will enrich the telling of biblical stories, especially for those storytellers who do not read scripture in the original language, so we encourage you to work from various translations.

Comments on the Stories

The specific contribution you will make to the preparation for telling one of these stories is your knowledge of your audience, knowing what will draw them into each story. Your familiarity with the audience will help you to know what aspects of the story to focus on, and will help you to be more creative in developing your own story line. You can take the information Mary Donovan Turner offers and shape a telling of the story that will be appropriate to the needs and life experiences of your group of listeners. Only you can know where in the lives of those in your congregation, class, or family a story will strike a chord, turn on a light, or heal a hurt. For more information on how to prepare a story for a specific group of listeners, refer to the chapter "Learning to Tell Bible Stories: A Self-directed Workshop" on pages 23-24.

Retelling the Stories

As a storyteller, you will contribute something of your own personality and understanding of the Bible and your listeners to the telling of a story based on a biblical text. There is no one right way to accomplish this task. While The Storyteller's Companion includes a sample retelling of each story, these retellings are only examples of one way a story may be told. You may choose to tell it very differently.

The retellings are intended to free your imagination for telling and not to limit you to any one form. Some retellings here are fairly straightforward recountings of a text. Others choose a character or characters from whose point of view to tell the story. Some retellings even place the story in the modern setting. We hope they will offer you a sample of the vast number of ways Bible stories can come to life in storytelling.

The goal of each retelling is to help our listeners to hear the wisdom of the lesson as if for the first time and to see the world of the lesson as something new and fresh. We are grateful for the imaginations of the storytellers who provided the retellings for this volume:

Mary Donovan Turner holds a Ph.D. from Emory University, where she studied Old Testament and Preaching. She is currently teaching at the Pacific School of Religion and the Graduate Theological Union. She is widely sought after as a preacher and lecturer. As editor of this volume I personally appreciate her determination and persistence as she overcame a brain tumor and significant loss of sight to write these comments.

R. Michael Sanders retold the stories based upon the texts from Isaiah. He is pastor of First United Methodist Church in Grayville, Illinois. He is the author of *The Pastor's Unauthorized Instruction Book* (Abingdon) and has written for various church periodicals including *The Door.*

Edward W. Thorn retold the stories based on Hosea, Amos, Micah, Habakkuk, and Zephaniah. He earned his Ph.D. at Indiana University. He taught for twenty years in the Communications Department of Florida Southern College. Currently, he is pastor of First United Methodist Church of Perry, Florida. He is the author of the forthcoming book *Hoof 'n Mouth Disease: Biblical Monologues and How to Do Them* (Lima, Ohio: C.S.S. Publishing).

Midrashim

If you ask a rabbi a question, you are likely to get a story for an answer. This reflects a wisdom that knows truth to be irreducible to a one-two-three answer. Truth is embodied in events as they happen and in persons as they relate to each other and to God. This kind of truth is best experienced in stories and concrete images. Perhaps no book is a better example of this storied truth telling than the Bible.

The most unique contribution The Storyteller's Companion makes to the art of biblical storytelling is to include the stories and sayings of the ancient rabbis related to the sayings of the prophets of the time leading up to the exile. These stories are called *midrashim* (the singular is *midrash*), from a Hebrew word that means "to go in search of." When the rabbis went in search of the relevance of these already "old, old stories" for their time, they returned with questions. Those questions generated stories that stand alongside the Scripture passages and interpret them in ways that children and adults alike are better able to understand.

The midrashim included here came from several sources, and I have retold and adapted them for inclusion here. You will find these midrashim in boxed text in the retelling of each story, placed near the part of the story to which they most closely relate. As you retell the story, you may wish to include one or more of the midrashim at these points in the story or at other appropriate places. For more information, refer to the chapter "What Are Midrashim, and What Are They Doing Here?" on pages 19-21.

You will probably not want to read this volume in The Storyteller's Companion to the Bible Series from front to back as you would most books. It is not designed to be read that way. One way to make effective use of this volume would be to read first Mary Donovan Turner's "A Narrative Introduction to the Pre-Exilic Prophets," on pages 15-17, and her comments on each of the stories and the introduction to midrash. Then choose a story that you wish to tell. This may be a story from an upcoming Sunday of the lectionary or the church school curriculum, or it may simply be a story that captures your interest. Once you have chosen the story, work through the short workshop on storytelling ("Learning to Tell Bible Stories: A Self-directed Workshop," pages 23-24), using the story you chose as your content. Practice telling your story alone until you feel comfortable.

As you tell the story to your group, notice which parts seem to touch your hearers the most. Take note of any questions or comments they may have, and incorporate these thoughts into any future stories.

Use the retelling provided with the story as a guide, but do not feel obligated to simply repeat it. Because you know your audience, you should tell the story for your hearers in your own way. You may choose to include the midrashim with your retelling, or you may tell them afterward, or you may choose not to include them at all. In any case, you are about to take part in one of the most ancient experiences people do in community: offering the gift of God's story so that it touches our story today.

A Narrative Introduction to the Pre-Exilic Prophets

Mary Donovan Turner

This volume of The Storyteller's Companion to the Bible deals with the canonical prophets whose primary body of work was pre-exilic. The sequence begins with Amos who was soon followed by Hosea; both were prophets to the Northern Kingdom of Israel in the eighth century B.C.E. These were succeeded by Micah and I Isaiah who prophesied in Judah during the same century. The late seventh century claims Zephaniah, Jeremiah, Nahum, Habakkuk, and parts of Ezekiel (covered in a separate Storyteller's volume). The use the lectionary makes of these prophets is interesting, and sometimes problematic. This series will focus on every lectionary reading (and alternate) coming from one of these eight prophetic books.

One might ask why a volume on storytelling would deal with the pre-exilic prophets. Admittedly only a very small segment of these works is narrative in form. Yet, it is important to remember that the spoken and penned prophetic word is an extremely important part of the story of Israel and Judah. Secondly, it is from the writings of the prophets that we can infer much of that same story.

Thus the prophetic word, at the same time, is part of the story *and* reflects the story of our ancestors. As storytellers, then, we find the pre-exilic prophets to be rich resources; we are challenged to discover the narrative buried latent within the texts.

While the pre-exilic prophets do exhibit some diversity in the genres they incorporate (one can find there call narratives, lawsuits, parables, songs, dirges, etc.), much of their corpus consists of accusations made against the nations by Yahweh through the prophetic word and consequent words of judgment. There are also scattered throughout words of promise and restoration. As a story-teller, one would wonder if this consistency and similarity between the books would stifle one's ability to bring a creative and distinctive word from each of the texts. Here the prophets have been quite kind to the storyteller, for while much of the text is accusation, threat, or promise, each prophet uses a particular set of metaphors and images to bring that word. Each metaphor and image opens a different narrative door. The common thematic elements running throughout the pre-exilic prophets—Yahweh's expectation for just, righteous, and faithful communities, the love of God that is extended to God's people in spite of their unfaithfulness, the deterioration of the covenant that will lead to national disaster and ruin—are brought to the hearer/reader in diverse, yet powerful, ways. This diversity becomes the fertile ground for the storyteller's imagination.

It is acknowledged that this volume is not methodologically consistent. The lectionary texts are examined through both historical and literary lenses. The inconsistency is part of the volume's design. There are a variety of questions that the storyteller can ask of a text that will yield the story that surrounds or is contained within the unit. Sometimes, for example, the key to the latent story in a text comes from examining the unit in its literary context. Often it comes from discerning the historical circumstances in which the text may have been written. Sometimes the story comes from an examination of the text's rhetoric, its manifold imagery, or, very often, its inconsistencies. This volume endeavors to demonstrate the various ways that our critical biblical methodologies enable us to bring a story to our own community of hearers.

We know very little about some of our pre-exilic prophets; when biographical information is sketchy or non-existent we must surmise from what they have written where they lived and why they felt compelled to bring a word from Yahweh. Other books in a straightforward manner and in narrative style bring a full and rich accounting of the joys and sorrows of prophethood. We know about *Amos* that he was from Tekoa in the hills of Judah. Amos went to the Northern Kingdom to deliver a word from Yahweh. He was a herder of sheep and a dresser of trees, and demonstrates an incredible solidarity with the poor of the land. Through poetic oracles and vision reports, he unrelentingly expresses Yahweh's demand for justice.

The counterpart of Amos in the Northern Kingdom was Hosea, whose writings betray a politically and religiously tumultuous time. The book of Hosea begins with an account of his marriage to Gomer, a perpetually unfaithful spouse. Through the story of their relationship, the reality of life between Yahweh and Yahweh's people comes to life. Hosea is concerned about unfaithfulness.

Isaiah, the first book of the "classical" prophets, indicates that the prophet brought the word of Yahweh during the last four decades of the eighth century B.C.E. The prophet was from Jerusalem; we are allowed to experience his own recounting of his prophetic call and his dealings with the aristocracy in Jerusalem. Isaiah was convinced that the future of the community was dependent on where it placed its trust and confidence. For Isaiah, trust belonged to Yahweh alone.

Micah, a younger contemporary of Isaiah, was a native of Moresheth, also in the Judean foothills. Micah launches attacks against the wealthy and against the corrupt rulers in Jerusalem.

We know little about the prophets Zephaniah and Habakkuk. We know only that Zephaniah prophesied during the reign of Josiah in the Southern Kingdom. Thematically he emphasizes God's great day of anger; he envisions a time when the whole earth will be destroyed. We know nothing about Habakkuk except what little we can infer from what he sees and the questions he asks. He sees violence, a consuming violence in his land. He asks God why.

It is in the recounting of the word of Jeremiah that we as readers come to know more intimately the life and times of a prophet of Yahweh. From the experience of his call to his final exile, we are allowed through poetry and narrative to feel the immense grief and tribulations of one called to bring the word of God to a nation unraveling and coming to its end. The book of Jeremiah contains his confessions, the stories about his rejection and alienation from the people he loved, and oracles depicting a God grieving over the future of a people bent on turning away.

From these accounts the storyteller is called to find those places where our own contemporary stories mirror *or* negate the stories found in the pre-exilic texts. It is a wondrous adventure.

What Are Midrashim, and What Are They Doing Here?

Michael E. Williams

Midrash (the plural in Hebrew is *midrashim)* comes from a Hebrew word meaning "to go in search of" or "to inquire." So midrashim resulted when the ancient rabbis went in search of (inquired into) the meaning of the Scriptures for their lives. Midrash is also the name for the process of inquiring into the Scriptures for their meaning.

We might say that midrash is both our encounter with the biblical stories as we seek their meaning for our lives and times and the stories that emerge to express that meaning. Often midrashim do take the form of stories or pieces of stories (at least the ones we will focus on here do). These stories seek to answer questions about and to fill gaps in the biblical stories.

The midrashim drawn from for this volume come from the period 400–1200 C.E. (what is sometimes called A.D.). Most of these midrashim originated in sermons preached in synagogues, based on the prescribed weekly readings from the Torah (the first five books of the Bible). Others emerged from the popular folk traditions of the Jewish communities. Though they were collected and written during that eight-hundred-year period, there is no way of knowing how long the midrashim had been circulating by word of mouth before someone wrote them down. Some are attributed to rabbis living at the time of Jesus. In fact, certain scholars find evidence that this way of interpreting the Bible has its roots intertwined with the texts of the biblical stories themselves.

I see three basic functions for the midrashim I have selected to be included in this book. The first might be called "filling the gaps." These stories and story fragments answer questions about the biblical stories that the Scripture leaves unanswered. When the rabbis answered such questions, they revealed both their fertile imaginations and their own understanding of God and human beings. Sunday school teachers and college professors will also have encountered these imaginative questions.

The second function of midrash is to draw an analogy. These stories begin with "This may be compared to. . . . " Then the rabbi would tell a contemporary story that exhibited a situation and characters like the biblical story under consideration. You may notice that these stories sometimes bear a resemblance to the parables of Jesus and the *mashal* (parable) form of Jewish teaching.

The third function is to describe an encounter. In these stories someone comes to a rabbi with a question, and the rabbi's response interprets both the biblical story and the situation from which the question emerged.

Why did I choose a predominantly Jewish form of interpretation in this book? First, Christians have too often ignored this ancient and time-honored way to interpret the Bible. Given our Jewish roots and Jesus' heritage, midrash is at least as directly related to our tradition as the Greco-Roman philosophy on which we have depended so heavily for ordering our questions and structuring our theological doctrines.

Second, midrashim provide us with a way of interpreting the Bible that involves the imagination and speaks to our experience. It is also, according to certain scholars, the way the Bible interprets itself.

Third, midrashim provide a model for a community-based, inclusive (even children can imaginatively participate in stories), nonprofessional (you don't have to be a trained theologian) way of interpreting the Bible for our times. In short, we can learn the stories the rabbis told about the scriptures to interpret them for their time. In addition, we can follow the example of the rabbis and learn to tell stories about Bible stories that interpret them for our time.

In addition to these reasons I have a personal appreciation for the Jewish storytelling tradition. My intellectual and artistic interests in Jewish narrative range from the Torah to midrash to hasidic stories to modern writers like Isaac Bashevis Singer and Elie Wiesel.

This is just the first step to reclaiming midrashim for modern tellers of Bible stories, but it is a step. If you want to learn more about midrashim related to the wisdom tradition, you may wish to read the volumes from which those included here were chosen.

Midrash Rabbah, translated by H. Freedman (London: Soncino Press, 1939), is a ten-volume translation of midrashim on a variety of books of the Bible. These references here, which have been paraphrased and adapted, are to chapter and section. The third edition of this work was published in 1983.

Volume one in Louis Ginzberg's classic collection of stories related to biblical texts, *The Legends of the Jews,* translated by Henrietta Szold (Philadelphia: The Jewish Publication Society, 1909 and 1937), still in print, draws from a wide number of sources, including Christian and Islamic traditions. Here this work, again paraphrased and adapted, is listed as Ginzberg, followed by the volume and page number.

A wonderful addition to the library of persons interested in midrashim is Rabbi William G. Braude's translation of Hayim Naham Bialik and Yehoshua Hana Ravnitzky's *The Book of Legends (Sefer Ha-Aggadah): Legends from the*

Talmud and Midrash. References to this work are cited as *Sefer Ha-Aggadah,* followed by the page number and section number.

One more word on midrash: For any given passage of Scripture, several stories or interpretations of various rabbis are presented side by side in collections of midrashim. Those who collected these stories saw no reason to decide which was the one right interpretation. This is also true, we might mention, of those who assembled the canon of the New Testament, who saw no reason to choose among the four very different stories about Rabbi Jesus. The understanding behind these choices is that there need be no single correct interpretation. The Bible is viewed as being so inclusive that it could apply to a range of possible life situations. Therefore, we would expect a variety of interpretations to speak to a variety of life situations. Not only the Bible, but also all of its many possible interpretations, are encompassed by the expansive imagination of God. In fact, Solomon, the wisest of all humans, is reputed by the rabbis to have known three thousand stories for every verse of Scripture and one thousand and five interpretations for every story.

Learning to Tell Bible Stories

A Self-directed Workshop

1. Read the story aloud at least twice. You may choose to read the translation included here or the one you are accustomed to reading. I recommend that you examine at least two translations as you prepare, so you can hear the differences in the way they sound when read aloud.

Do read them *aloud*. Yes, if you are not by yourself, people may give you funny looks, but this really is important. Your ear will hear things about the passage that your eye will miss. Besides, you can't skim when you read aloud. You are forced to take your time, and you might notice aspects of the story that you never saw (or heard) before.

As you read, pay special attention to *where* the story takes place, *when* the story takes place, *who* the characters are, *what* objects are important to the story, and the general *order of events* in the story.

2. Now close your eyes and imagine the story taking place. This is your chance to become a playwright/director or screenwriter/filmmaker because you will experience the story on the stage or screen in your imagination. Enjoy this part of the process. It takes only a few minutes, and the budget is within everybody's reach.

3. Look back at the story briefly to make sure you haven't left out any important people, places, things, or events.

4. Try telling the story. This works better if you have someone to listen (even the family pet will do). You can try speaking aloud to yourself or to an imaginary listener. Afterward ask your listener or yourself what questions arise as a result of this telling. Is the information you need about the people, places, things, or language in the story? Is it appropriate to the age, experiences, and interests of those who will be hearing it? Does the story capture your imagination? One more thing: You don't have to be able to explain the meaning of a story to tell it. In fact, those of the most enduring interest have an element of mystery about them.

5. Read the "Comments on the Story" that Mary Donovan Turner has provided for each passage. Are some of your questions answered there? You may wish also to look at a good Bible dictionary for place names, characters, professions, objects, or worlds that you need to learn more about. *The Interpreter's Dictionary of the Bible* (Nashville: Abingdon Press, 1962) is still the most complete source for storytellers.

6. Read the "Retelling the Story" section for the passage you are learning to tell. Does it give you any ideas about how you will tell the story? How would you tell it differently? Would you tell it from another character's point of view? How would that make it a different story? Would you transfer it to a modern setting? What places and characters will you choose to correspond to those in the biblical story? Remember, the retellings that are provided are not meant to be told exactly as they are written here. They are to serve as springboards for your imagination as you develop your telling.

7. Read the midrashim that accompany each retelling. Would you include any of these in your telling? You could introduce them by saying, "This is not in the original story, but the rabbis say. . . . " Do these midrashim respond to any of your questions or relate to any of your life situations or those of your listeners? If so, you might consider using them after the retelling to encourage persons to tell their own stories, which hearing the Bible story has brought to mind. You may even wish to begin creating some modern midrashim of your own or with your listeners.

8. Once you have gotten the elements of the story in mind and have chosen the approach you are going to take in retelling it, you need to practice, practice, practice. Tell the story aloud ten or twenty or fifty times over a period of several days or weeks. Listen as you tell your story. Revise your telling as you go along. Remember that you are not memorizing a text; you are preparing a living event. Each time you tell the story, it will be a little different, because you will be different (if for no other reason than that you have told the story before).

9. Then "taste and see" that even the stories of God are good—not all sweet, but good and good for us and for those who hunger to hear.

Come, Let Us Argue

The prophet, like a prosecutor, summons the whole universe into his amphitheatre and indicts the rebellious children of Judah and Jerusalem for grieving their heavenly parent.

The Story

THE vision which Isaiah son of Amoz had about Judah and Jerusalem during the reigns of Uzziah, Jotham, Ahaz, and Hezekiah, kings of Judah.

Let the heavens and the earth give
    ear,
for it is the LORD who speaks:
I reared children and brought them
    up,
but they have rebelled against me.
An ox knows its owner
and a donkey its master's stall;
but Israel lacks all knowledge,
my people has no discernment.
You sinful nation, a people weighed
    down with iniquity,
a race of evildoers, children whose
    lives are depraved,
who have deserted the LORD,
spurned the Holy One of Israel,
and turned your backs on him!
Why do you invite more punishment,
why persist in your defection?
Your head is all covered with sores,
your whole body is bruised;
from head to foot there is not a
    sound spot in you—
nothing but weals and welts and raw
    wounds
which have not felt compress or
    bandage
or the soothing touch of oil.
Your country is desolate, your cities
    burnt down.

Before your eyes strangers devour
    your land;
it is as desolate as Sodom after its
    overthrow.
Only Zion is left,
like a watchman's shelter in a
    vineyard,
like a hut in a plot of cucumbers,
like a beleaguered city.
Had the LORD of Hosts not left us a
    few survivors,
we should have become like Sodom,
no better than Gomorrah.
Listen to the word of the LORD, you
    rulers of Sodom;
give ear to the teaching of our God,
    you people of Gomorrah:
Your countless sacrifices, what are
    they to me?
says the LORD.
I am sated with whole-offerings of
    rams
and the fat of well-fed cattle;
I have no desire for the blood of
    bulls,
of sheep, and of he-goats,
when you come into my presence.
Who has asked you for all this?
No more shall you tread my courts.
To bring me offerings is futile;
the reek of sacrifice is abhorrent to
    me.
New moons and sabbaths and sacred
    assemblies—

such idolatrous ceremonies I cannot
endure.
I loathe your new moons and your
festivals;
they have become a burden to me,
and I can tolerate them no longer.
When you hold out your hands in
prayer,
I shall turn away my eyes.
Though you offer countless prayers,
I shall not listen;
there is blood on your hands.
Wash and be clean;
put away your evil deeds
far from my sight;
cease to do evil, learn to do good.

Pursue justice, guide the
oppressed;
uphold the rights of the fatherless,
and plead the widow's cause.

Now come, let us argue this out,
says the LORD.
Though your sins are scarlet,
they may yet be white as snow;
though they are dyed crimson,
they may become white as wool.
If you are willing to obey,
you will eat the best that earth
yields;
but if you refuse and rebel,
the sword will devour you.
The LORD himself has spoken.

Comments on the Story

These oracles in Isaiah provide for the reader the starting place, the beginning, perhaps the rationale for "first" Isaiah (chapters 1–39) in its entirety. Harsh words are brought to the people of Judah and Jerusalem who have become estranged from Yahweh. The words are brought through Isaiah, son of Amoz, who summons all of heaven and earth to hear what he has seen. The prophet desperately calls out for the world to listen. Perhaps the urgency in his voice is enough to produce a "hush" across the heavens and earth, much like the hush that settles across the courtroom when the judge enters and the charges are brought against the defendant. The superscription that identifies the prophet (1:1) and the following introductory unit (1:2-20), the words from this Isaiah, are not explicitly narrative in style; the unit is comprised of a series of oracles from Yahweh. Nevertheless, the contemporary storyteller will have no difficulty recounting a multitude of stories that illustrate in human dimension the agony of Yahweh who grieves over the severed relationship Yahweh has with the people of Judah.

As the chapter begins, the careful reader notices that a predominant metaphor is used to depict the relationship between Yahweh and the people—a parent/child metaphor. Yahweh has reared the children (v. 2) and brought them up. The people are described as offspring who do evil and children who deal corruptly (v. 4). Yahweh witnesses the people living in self-destructive, unproductive ways. The question Yahweh then asks is one that we understand. It is the question asked by any parent who feels that the child has become a stranger (v. 4) or the question asked by anyone who feels betrayed by someone they have loved—*Why* (v. 5)?

The imagery of the oracles moves subtly between that of the fractured relationship between parent and child to that of the land—the desolate, devoured, overthrown, besieged land (vv. 7-9). The description of the wounded child and the wounded land forms the backdrop for the series of complaints Yahweh has against the people that Yahweh has reared. What is the complaint? It is one of dishonesty and of shallow allegiance. The people have performed their rituals and made their sacrifices, yet the sacrifices are not *wholly* satisfying to Yahweh who finds them to be an abomination. They cannot be endured. They are hated; they are a burden (vv. 12-14). Yahweh is weary from them because the one who prays has hands *"full of blood"* (v. 15 RSV). The picture of the praying one who has on his hands the blood of the dying poor, the blood of the forgotten and the oppressed, provides for the storyteller a pathetic image that can easily be brought to life—an image all too familiar—an image of shallow devotion and hypocritical posture.

In four-fold fashion, the parent pleads with the children to put behind them their unfaithful ways; they are implored to wash, make themselves clean, remove evil, and cease doing evil (v. 16). Additionally, the people are called to put on faithful ways; they are implored to learn to do good, seek justice, rescue the oppressed, defend the orphan, and plead for the widow (v. 17). To know the will of the parent is not to make superficial sacrifice; to make sacrifice and to assemble together for festivals and feast days is far too easy. To be Yahweh's people requires much more; it is to learn to do good in the world where one lives. To be Yahweh's people means to seek the well-being of all, of each and every member of the community.

Is the story of Israel a comedy or a tragedy? Whether or not this first text in Isaiah leaves us with a sense of hopefulness or hopelessness, with possibility or despair, depends on how far we read. Does the story end in verse 15? There Yahweh, weary of the shallow devotion of the people, is ready to turn away and avert eyes from the unfaithful ones. The story would end with Yahweh's refusal to listen to their prayers, with the parent's disappointment and anger at the behavior of the children and with the parent lashing out at the child, detailing the offenses and demanding reform. But the editor of Isaiah 1 does not leave us there. There is an additional word from the parent to the child: "Come now, let us argue (reason) it out, says the LORD" (v. 18 NRSV). Even now the final word is for reconciliation. The final request is for dialogue. Argument is relationship continued, and the parent describes the potential for restoration. "Though your sins are like scarlet, they shall be like snow" (v. 18 NRSV). It is a magnificent offer, though there are, of course, remaining conditions. The children must be willing and obedient, and it is the only way they can prosper. Not to live in life-producing ways means death (v. 20), but the people continue to have a choice.

Isaiah 1:1-20 does not end in resolution. The text is a prelude to many passages that relate harsh words of indictment and threat against the unfaithful people of God. While there is no resolution, however, the text does end in possibility. *If* the people come and join in the conversation, there is hope.

Yahweh's initial question is never answered. Never in the prophetic word is there a clear understanding of *why* the children have strayed. The question of motive continues occasionally to plague both Yahweh and Isaiah and the prophets who follow him. *Why* is the enduring question. In this text it remains a mystery, but the eighth-century prophet continues to watch and name the unfaithfulness that he sees. He continues to watch the events of the world unfold before his eyes and to ask—How are we as the people of God to interpret what is happening in light of Yahweh's purpose and hopes and dreams for us? The very name Isaiah, which means "Yahweh gives salvation," names that hope—that the people of Israel will continue the conversation with Yahweh and be saved. The storyteller is invited to end the story with an air of possibility . . . only possibility.

Retelling the Story

The City and its outlying farms was a place like no other, a place where the past persisted alongside the present, and modern thought gave place to ancient ways. On this day it was Mother's Day, a secular holiday for some, a religious holiday for others.

> The ancient sages compare the disobedient people to a king's son who played hooky from school after his father had told him explicitly to attend classes. The son chose, rather, to play in the street with his friends. When the king learned of his son's disobedience he scolded the youngster soundly. After the scolding, though, the king invited his son to wash his hands and dine with his father. That is why the passage from Isaiah opened with God's lament over the people's disobedience and ended with the invitation to come and discuss (argue or reason) what has taken place. (*Exodus Rabbah 25.29-30*)

From the porch steps of her white frame farmhouse Amah shaded her eyes to look up the dusty road at the approaching delivery van. Neat painted letters read "Johnson's Florist" as the green van pulled into her drive and stopped. David Johnson struggled out from behind the wheel of the van. He limped to open the van's back doors and then pulled out a tissue wrapped basket of flowers. She pitied David's progress toward her on his once-burned limbs, now recovered as much as they ever would. With the angelic side of his face turned toward her he smiled, "They're from Paul, Amah!" Still she glimpsed the ragged other side of his smile with the lips that could never quite close. Then David was gone, van and all disappearing in the hovering dust.

Of course the flowers were from Paul. She had no other child but Paul, who had come with the spring with his dark almond eyes and legs that resisted swaddling. Paul was her unexpected gift from God, a still-wet newborn left in the City's marketplace, as unwanted children had always been. An early-rising man of God had spied the child before the slave traders and the dogs, and thinking of Amah's farm, the rooms that echoed, and her widowhood, he brought Paul to her. "Yahweh-loves-you-little-Paul" she had sung to him, wanting from the beginning to breathe her very faith into him. Ribbons trailing from his cradleboard repeated her promise, "Given to Yahweh."

She had fenced in the yard for his toddling feet, making sure the posts were splinter-free, and the gate secure. But even then Paul soon lost interest in his swing and his pool. He laced his still-plump fingers through the gate and shook it crying "Out, Mah!" Too soon Paul learned to climb the fence, and the sheltering farm with its twelve-stone altar became his world. On clear nights from the porch swing she answered his questions about God.

Much too soon Paul went to the City for school, boarding there during the week. As he grew, whether she pleaded or punished, Paul's arguments echoed his infant desire "out." As a youth at the high place he embraced the idol worshiped by his young friends, or at least its surrogate. He tattooed his flesh with its symbols and his soul with its rites. He took drugs, and as a young man drank heavily. When Paul came to visit the farm bringing her gifts on other Mother's Days, Amah wondered how it was that her son knew nothing, and why he had rebelled.

Paul had gone to live in the City with a young woman who had a little daughter not quite two. Paul watched the child while her mother worked. One day, drunken beyond reason and annoyed by the girl's incessant crying, Paul had shaken the child until she was silent; she fell asleep and never awoke. Paul had been tried and convicted of the child's murder, but the judge had not yet imposed sentence.

Amah sat on the porch with Paul's flowers, their sickening sweet odor blending with the scent of funeral flowers that still seemed to fill her nostrils. Paul had written on the card, "Mah, you must come and testify for me at the sentencing hearing. Tell the judge you don't believe I meant to do it. It wasn't my fault, Mah. I was drunk."

Later, in the evening's cool she took stationery from her writing desk and went out on the porch to write. "Why do you send me flowers, Paul? I have

The rabbis said that God offers the people two roads to follow. They compare this to a master offering a servant the choice between a necklace made of gold, or chains made of iron. Though it seems lacking in good sense, on numerous occasions people choose the chains and slavery of security instead of the golden promises of God. (*Deuteronomy Rabbah 4.2*) not asked for them. Your gifts disgust me. They lie heavy on my soul. You are asking for my help but I will not listen to you. Your hands are covered with blood. Take your wrongdoing out of my sight. Cease to do evil, learn to do good, and seek justice. Let us talk this over, you and I. Your sin can be made white as snow. If you are willing to obey, you will have the good things of life but if you keep on rebelling, God's judgment will have you instead."

(R. Michael Sanders)

The Urgent Invitation

The cultures are at war, and it is time that we go to the mountain to make peace.

The Story

This is the message which Isaiah son of Amoz received in a vision about Judah and Jerusalem.

In days to come
the mountain of the LORD's house
will be set over all other mountains,
raised high above the hills.
All the nations will stream towards
it,
and many peoples will go and say,
'Let us go up to the mountain of the
LORD,
to the house of the God of Jacob,
that he may teach us his ways
and that we may walk in his
paths.'

For instruction comes from Zion,
and the word of the LORD from
Jerusalem.
He will judge between the nations
as arbiter among many peoples.
They will beat their swords into
mattocks
and their spears into pruning-knives;
nation will not lift sword against
nation
nor ever again be trained for war.
Come, people of Jacob,
let us walk in the light of the LORD.

Comments on the Story

Rarely does a story have two beginnings. A story begins and either meanders along or rushes impetuously to its conclusion. Rarely do we read "once upon a time" only to read those words again some pages or chapters later!

But that is what happens in the book of Isaiah. The "story" begins first in chapter 1 when the editor identifies the prophet who has seen the word of Yahweh concerning Judah and Jerusalem and who then feels compelled to share that word with the community of Yahweh's people. Then, in chapter 2, the story begins again. The introduction is not as elaborate as the first, but the identified prophet is the same. It is Isaiah, son of Amoz, who sees the word of Yahweh. Immediately the editor moves from the identification of the speaker to words spoken.

The oracle in chapter 1 began with the words "Let the heavens and the earth give ear, for it is the LORD who speaks." The introduction, as we have noted, was prelude to a poetic exhortation and indictment against the community.

However, in chapter 2, the oracle begins with the phrase "in days to come" (v. 2). Unlike the familiar beginning to our fairy tales, "once upon a time," and unlike the beginning of Isaiah 1, which turns our attention to the past and present, the reader is alerted in chapter 2 to turn her attention to the future. *In days to come,* this is what will happen. The reader's interest is piqued; what is it that will happen in Judah and Jerusalem? Will this be a nightmare—another depiction of a desolate and forsaken land? Will there again be images of destruction and death? Will accusations and invectives once again be hurled at the people of Judah? Will what is "to come" be reminiscent of chapter 1, the first beginning to this "story"? No. This is a dream about a new age, pregnant with possibility and rich with promise.

It will not be difficult for the storyteller to bring to the community in narrative form the essence of this new age, these rich words of hope. The picture painted for us by the prophet draws our eye to the peak of a mountain—Yahweh's mountain—the highest mountain, higher than any of the hills that surround it. The storyteller can describe a mountain, which by its powerful presence invites people to journey toward it—"Let us go up to the mountain of the LORD" (v. 3).

What will be so enticing about this place, this mountain? Is it simply its height, its power, its beauty that draws people there? No, of course not. There must be more. There must be a *promise* tied to this mountain. People will travel great distances on the power of a promise, particularly this one. This is a promise of peace.

The onslaught of the media that incessantly invades our lives provides contemporary storytellers with a bounteous assortment of images—people who would travel anywhere to find peace. Daily we witness the furrowed brows and vacant eyes of those who live every day with the fear that, because of war, this day may be their last. They are hungry. The fields are destroyed, the crops are gone. There seems to be a choice, an either/or. Either there is famine and war *or* there is peace and nourishment for themselves, and for the children. With their last ounce of energy, carrying ones they love who can no longer make the journey, they would indeed travel toward this mountain rising high into the heavens *if* there was at the mountain the promise of peace.

Zion is this mountain of God, the house of Yahweh; it is the place of promise. It is the place where the peoples of the world can learn Yahweh's ways, the instruction, the word of the Lord. Yahweh will judge and settle the disputes for the nations. There will be no more need for weapons; the swords will be beaten into plows and once again the children's stomachs gnarled from hunger will be filled. There will be no more need for spears; they will be beaten into pruning hooks as men and women once again work in the fields, bringing in the bountiful harvest that God will provide for them. That is the promise—that never again will a sword from one nation be lifted against another. Never again will the peoples of the earth learn war (v. 4).

Perhaps, we think, the vision is too good to be true, but even the most remote possibility that it could be true makes the journey to the mountain worthwhile. The internal and urgent invitation pours out of the mouths of those who see the mountain in the distance. "Let us go up to the mountain" they first declare upon seeing the great mountain rising in the distance (v. 3). Again, they say, "Come, . . . let us walk in the light of the LORD" (v. 5).

The promise is so wonderful, one wonders how *they* could have refused it. And yet they did. The remainder of chapter 2 gives testimony to the choices the people of Judah and Jerusalem made. Their choice was not to travel to the mountain, not to know the ways of Yahweh, not to be instructed in the ways of peace. The city is filled with the haughty and the proud, and the day that will come will not be one of peace. The coming day of Yahweh is one of terror (vv. 20-22).

The promise is so wonderful, one wonders how *we* can refuse it.

And yet we do. The media gives testimony to the choices that we as God's people continue to make. We decide not to travel toward the mountain, even though the place of Yahweh promises peace. The contemporary storyteller can paint the picture of peace and enable the community to "catch hold of the vision." The storyteller can help us experience the urgent invitation anew.

Retelling the Story

He had come to the Mountain. He was a soldier, a veteran of the City's wars, with scars inside and outside to vouch for his patriotism. The war against the enemies of the City ended, but his war had not. He knew no other way. Fists, weapons—these things settled scores and brought him the illusion of security. But the illusion of security brought no peace or joy. There had to be something better. Didn't there?

So he came to the shrine on the Mountain. The Prophet had spoken of a place, a time when wars would end. The City was at peace, her enemies weak, scattered, or bought off. But there was no peace. Young men still

The sages say that the Bible gives clues to the lineage of a prophet, if one has eyes to see them. If the Bible lists the father's name as well as the son, then the father was a prophet also, according to them. There is an exception, though. The rabbis tell that Amos's father was a prophet, even though his name is never mentioned. You can also discern the city of a prophet's origin by means of biblical clues. If a prophet's hometown is not mentioned, then the prophet hails from Jerusalem. It just made sense to them that the majority of holy people would come from the holy city. (*Sefer Ha-Aggadah* 475.67) trained for war, the smiths and technicians still produced weapons. And the heart of this veteran was still at war, but the only enemies were business competitors, neighbors who built too close to his property and a wife he fought even as he loved her.

He came upon the shrine in the mid-afternoon, the sun blazed, hot as his hate. He could not control the sun any more than he could stop his warring heart.

There was no one there. No attendant to take his offerings or to offer him temptation. No long lines to wait in and no great columned temples. The shrine was set in a wall of stone, crudely chiseled out of the hard granite. He smiled without humor at the thought that the words were literally "carved in the stone."

The veteran ran his calloused hand over each word, reading them with his eyes and touch.

> He shall judge between the nations
> and shall arbitrate for many peoples;
> they shall beat their swords into plow-
>   shares,
> and their spears into pruning hooks;
> nation shall not lift up sword against
>   nation,
> neither shall they learn war any more.

The rabbis described the self-limiting nature of God in geographical terms. God's voice could be heard in any land before Israel was chosen. Afterward, God chose only to speak in Eretz Israel. Before there was a Temple, God's presence pervaded Jerusalem. After the Temple was built, God's presence resided there. They do not go on to say where God chose to speak after Israel was no more, or where God's presence resided after the destruction of the Temple. Who knows? Perhaps things came full circle and God's presence and voice were available to communities across the globe once again. (*Sefer Ha-Aggadah* 363.45)

These were only words. He should have laughed at them. He was a veteran of so many battles. He saw nothing happening that would vindicate such a pronouncement. He knew that the smiths still prepared weapons and generals worked out scenarios. The warring madness of the City, of all cities, seemed to have no end in sight. But he felt the stirring in his soul. Deep within that scarred psyche, something he thought he had killed long ago was resurrected. He felt hope for the first time in years.

Why? What in those crude words touched him so?

He read the words again. It was the word *shall* that arrested his attention. Yes, there it was again and again! Five times that word appeared. What had his language teacher taught him so long ago in his youth? What was it Mrs. Davis said about the word "shall"?

"Shall is the strongest word in our language," he heard her say again. "Shall gives place to no doubts, no conditions for the occurrence, no room for alternate views. Shall means it will absolutely come to pass."

The veteran stared for a moment longer, beginning to understand his hope and the source of his hope. Then he began to believe. The Prophet had spoken the word of God and the word was "Shall." No doubt, no conditions, just the promise of the One Who Cannot Lie. *(R. Michael Sanders)*

I Loved and Lost

A farmer sings a love song to his vineyard, but the vineyard bears wild fruit. Why?

The Story

I shall sing for my beloved
my love song about his vineyard:
My beloved had a vineyard
high up on a fertile slope.
He trenched it, cleared it of stones,
and planted it with choice red
vines;
in the middle he built a watch-tower
and also hewed out a wine vat.
He expected it to yield choice grapes,
but all it yielded was a crop of wild
grapes.

Now, you citizens of Jerusalem
and people of Judah,
judge between me and my vineyard.
What more could have been done for
my vineyard
than I did for it?
Why, when I expected it to yield
choice grapes,

did it yield wild grapes?
Now listen while I tell you
what I am about to do to my
vineyard:
I shall take away its hedge
and let it go to waste,
I shall break down its wall
and let it be trampled underfoot;
I shall leave it derelict.
It will be neither pruned nor hoed,
but left overgrown with briars and
thorns.
I shall command the clouds
to withhold their rain from it.
The vineyard of the LORD of Hosts is
Israel,
Judah the plant he cherished.
He looked for justice but found
bloodshed,
for righteousness but heard cries of
distress.

Comments on the Story

It is not just a story about a farmer and the crop. It is a love song, a love song about a love gone awry. How many love songs end in a cry of despair? Many. Relationships are filled with promises and disappointments.

The love song comes in the form of a parable; some say it is an allegory. It is a narrative nonetheless that tells the story of the farmer who, with great expectation and anticipation, goes out to ready the land for a bountiful crop. The expectations for bounty are neither idealistic nor unrealistic. The farmer plants the vineyard on a very fertile hill (v. 1). There is every likelihood that the crop will be planted; it will grow and come to fruition. Not that the farmer is willing to leave the outcome to chance! Everything possible is done to

36

insure the bountiful harvest. The farmer digs the land and clears away the stones that could thwart the growth of the precious vines; there could be no hindrance to its productivity. Not just any vines were planted—only the most choice were used. A tower is placed in the field to keep unwanted animals from destroying the crop. The field would be supervised. What could go wrong? A strong crop is virtually guaranteed, and the wine vat is hewed out in the field because there is every expectation that excellent grapes would appear.

The story begins with a great sense of expectation and anticipation. The prophet begins singing a love song about dedication and commitment, but soon Yahweh joins in (v. 3), and the song changes from major to minor key, from harmony to dissonance; the exuberant lyrics become bitter and forlorn. The audience is asked to "judge" between the farmer and the vineyard. All is not well, and it is Yahweh who sings of the disastrous and unanticipated results of the farmer's efforts. The field does not yield good grapes but wild grapes. Yahweh passionately pours out the frustration and lack of understanding to those who are hearing the song. Yahweh at the same time asks and pleads, "What more could have been done for my vineyard?" (v. 4). The unstated response is, of course, there is nothing. Again, as in Isaiah 1, the farmer asks—Why? Why, when I took every precaution did the field yield wild grapes, grapes not capable of making good wine?

Those hearing the story would surely pass judgment. There is no explanation for the failed crop; the farmer has done all that is possible. And the farmer's response to this failed crop? Yes, the hearers would think, it is the logical one. The field has not produced as it could have, and thus the farmer removes its protection, breaks down its walls. The harvest season is over; the crop is trampled. It cannot be used; the field has not fulfilled its purpose. The audience would agree; to abandon the field is the logical response.

But alas! The audience has passed judgment on themselves! *They* are the field so rich with promise. They were planted in the most fertile of places; Yahweh thought them to be the choicest of vines. Yahweh had expected them to be productive, but because they were not, the song turns into a very troubling song of violence and despair. Emotions are raw and wounds are deep because, as we have come to realize, this is not just a story about a farmer and a crop. It is a love story about Yahweh and Yahweh's people. Yahweh has loved them and nurtured them; Yahweh saw in them the potential for a faithful relationship that would last forever. In front of the world, Yahweh made a commitment to them, but in vain. And Yahweh tramples the field and makes it a waste. Yahweh acknowledges that his hopes were naive and his dreams misguided; Yahweh is the jilted lover.

We can empathize with the violence and despair. We are surrounded by stories, both real and imagined, about people who passionately invest themselves in relationships that ultimately hurt and disappoint them. We know about the potential pain of making ourselves vulnerable to ones we love. Such is the story of Yahweh. Yahweh loved the people and expected from them nothing less than *justice* and *righteousness* (v. 7). But instead of justice, Yahweh saw bloodshed. Instead of righteousness, Yahweh heard the cries from those Yahweh loved—cries from those who are oppressed because the world had not yet learned to live in life-giving ways.

Chapter 5 continues. The love song is over. Yahweh becomes silent, but the prophet speaks—reiterating the piercing cries from the world gone awry, the cries from those Yahweh has loved. The six-fold cries of mourning, of sorrow and lament, (see vv. 8, 11, 18, 20, 21, 22; and also 10:1) come from those who are not living just and righteous lives. Each cry begins a unit that provides a rich and provocative image for the storyteller of life gone wrong. There are those who have no room in their homes for others (v. 8), who do not regard the deeds of Yahweh (v. 12), who call evil good and good evil and who are wise in their own eyes (vv. 20-21), and those who deprive the innocent of their rights (v. 23). The community is not a community. Those who live life this way do not love Yahweh.

And so the story comes to an end. It is not the only story in the Old Testament; in many places Yahweh picks up the tune and begins to sing once again to and for the people Yahweh loves. But not here. In this "song of the vineyard" Isaiah invites the storyteller to ponder and present to the listening community the portrait of a God deeply invested in the lives of the people that God has created, a God who has high expectations for the covenant people and who gives to them all that they need to flourish and live fertile and productive lives, a God who experiences great remorse and anger and anguish for the many ways the people continue to be disappointing. The storyteller can depict the heartbroken God, one whose anger at the same time makes us uncomfortable and encourages us to ask important questions. Wouldn't we want our God to be offended by injustice? Do we not depend on and expect God to hear, see, and then act against oppression? Perhaps the answer to that question depends on whether we see ourselves as the oppressed or the oppressor.

Retelling the Story

Amah had fed and watered the livestock and scattered feed for the chickens even earlier that morning than usual. Then she had washed and put on a cool cotton sari, braiding her hair into a single long plait that hung down her back. She packed a basket with that summer's blackberry jam and a loaf of fresh baked bread and set off walking the three miles to the City. With feet that knew the road, Amah had no need to note the way, but fixed her eyes on the cloudless blue vault of sky over the City's acropolis. Almost it seemed to her that she could walk right into that sky and into the very presence of God. It was a word from God that Amah was seeking and she was going to visit the prophetess Joanna to find it.

The prophetess lived on the twentieth floor of the City's newest high-rise apartment building in a simple efficiency unit with a small aislelike balcony and white walls unadorned by any moulding. At Amah's knock, Joanna opened the door and let Amah inside. With fragile, aged hands Joanna accepted the gifts of bread and jam and asked Amah to join her on the balcony. Joanna sat and then Amah. In deference to Amah's obvious grief, Joanna said nothing. An hour passed before Amah could explain that her beloved only child, Paul, had chosen to worship the City's idol and had further polluted himself with drunkenness and immorality. Amah recounted how in drunken anger Paul had shaken a child so that she died and that Paul had been convicted of murder. "Today," Amah grieved, "Paul will be sentenced and I must decide if I will testify at his sentencing hearing." Then Amah was silent.

For a long time Joanna was also silent and then turning her delicate black face up she began to chant a lament. "Let me sing a song of my friend's love for her farm. Yes! My friend had only one acre in a well-drained valley. She tilled that acre, piling its stones in neat fences. In its fertile soil she planted choice walnut seedlings. These she tended for many years, even all the years it takes to raise a boy-child to manhood. Because she tended them faithfully she expected those trees would yield good walnuts. But wizened kernels were all they gave." Then with tears finding established courses down her wrinkled cheeks Joanna looked to see if Amah had understood.

One of the rabbis told this story concerning God's conversation with Moses about the children of Israel. Once there was a king whose vineyard was cared for by a tenant. When the wine that the vineyard produced was good, the king would claim credit saying, "My what fine wine my vineyard produces." Whenever the wine turned out to be sour the king would say to the tenant, "Your wine is terrible." Finally, the tenant told the king, "When the wine is good you claim it for your own but when the wine is bad I am blamed. You know that whether sour or sweet, the vineyard, the grapes, and the wine are yours."

Just so when the people sinned and God asked Moses what he was going to do with those people he (Moses) brought out of Egypt. Moses replied, "So when the people don't sin you say that they are yours, but when they go astray and sin greatly you say that they are mine. Still, they are your people whether they sin or not. So, what are *you* going to do with these people *you* brought out of Egypt?" (*Sefer Ha-Aggadah* 343.77)

It is recorded in the criminal records of the City that Amah the sorrowing mother of Paul stood before the judge that afternoon and said: "People of the City and this honorable judge, I ask you to judge between my son and me. What could I have done for my son that I did not do? I expected him to become an upright man who practiced mercy and feared God. Instead he has shed blood and caused cries of distress. Very well, I will not ask for the rain of mercy for my chosen son. I am removing the hedge from around him that I used to be. Let him become like a garden laid waste, unpruned, undug, overgrown by weeds." And the People greatly wondered at Amah's love for her son. *(R. Michael Sanders)*

Without three things the world would not continue in existence, say the sages. The first of these is justice. The second thing is truth. And, finally, the third is peace. Without the presence of these three qualities in life the world would cease to be. (*Sefer Ha-Aggadah* 690.1)

When Ordinary Words Won't Do

A prophet is called to ministry, and he accepts the challenge, "Send me!" He is compelled, however, to deliver a message that will not please his hearers.

The Story

IN the year that King Uzziah died I saw the Lord seated on a throne, high and exalted, and the skirt of his robe filled the temple. Seraphim were in attendance on him. Each had six wings: with one pair of wings they covered their faces and with another their bodies, and with the third pair they flew. They were calling to one another,

'Holy, holy, holy is the LORD of
  Hosts:
the whole earth is full of his glory.'

As each called, the threshold shook to its foundations at the sound, while the house began to fill with clouds of smoke. Then I said,

'Woe is me! I am doomed,
for my own eyes have seen the King,
  the LORD of Hosts,
I, a man of unclean lips,
I, who dwell among a people of
  unclean lips.'

One of the seraphim flew to me, carrying in his hand a glowing coal which he had taken from the altar with a pair of tongs. He touched my mouth with it and said,

'This has touched your lips;
now your iniquity is removed
and your sin is wiped out.'

I heard the Lord saying, 'Whom shall I send? Who will go for us?'

I said: 'Here am I! Send me.' He replied: 'Go, tell this people:

However hard you listen, you will
  never understand.
However hard you look, you will
  never perceive.
This people's wits are dulled;
they have stopped their ears and
  shut their eyes,
so that they may not see with their
  eyes,
nor listen with their ears,
nor understand with their wits,
and then turn and be healed.'

I asked, 'Lord, how long?' And he answered,

'Until cities fall in ruins and are
  deserted,
until houses are left without
  occupants,
and the land lies ruined and
  waste.'
The LORD will drive the people far
  away,
and the country will be one vast
  desolation.
Even though a tenth part of the
  people were to remain,
they too would be destroyed
like an oak or terebinth
when it is felled,
and only a stump remains.
Its stump is a holy seed.

41

Comments on the Story

Sometimes ordinary words just won't do. Ordinary words can't capture intense fear, the beauty of a magnificent sunset, or the love for a child. Ordinary words could not capture the experience of Isaiah when he received his call to be a prophet for Yahweh.

The time is the year King Uzziah died, 742 B.C.E. King Uzziah had reigned forty-one years in Judah and by the harsh standards of the royal world, he had been quite successful. He had repaired the defenses of Jerusalem, reorganized the army, and secured the many trade routes running through Judah. He was strong, but died, the Chronicler tells us (26:1-21) punished by Yahweh for his proud power. It was in the year that he died, when the country was mourning his passing, wondering what the future would bring, that Isaiah saw his vision.

The place is the temple. We are not surprised by the setting—we expect such things to happen in the temple. We do not, perhaps, expect visions of thrones or winged seraphs who sing about the holiness and glory of God. We do not expect the shaking of the thresholds, and we do not expect smoke rising to the heights. These are not ordinary words describing ordinary things, but ordinary words often cannot be used to describe one's encounter with God.

Isaiah is standing in the temple when he sees the vision of Yahweh sitting on a throne. Yahweh is high and lifted up. The seraphs are singing to one another words that we have often sung, "Holy, holy, holy is the LORD. . . . " The building shakes, the smoke rises, and Isaiah speaks.

It is not in response to Yahweh's call that we hear Isaiah's first words, for Yahweh has not yet spoken. The first words of Isaiah come in response to the remarkable vision he has experienced, and his first words are words of despair—"Woe is me!" In contrast to the greatness witnessed, Isaiah feels small. In contrast to glory (a weighty splendor) and holiness (something very distant from the ordinary), Isaiah feels unclean. Isaiah feels that he has no place in the presence of one as awesome as this. The reader of Old Testament narrative is familiar with the fear and awe that go in tandem with seeing Yahweh. Repeatedly the Israelites asked, "Can one see Yahweh and live?" Isaiah seems not so occupied with death as he is with *how he has lived life*. He has unclean lips; the community of which he is a part has unclean lips.

It is the seraph who responds to the outburst of Isaiah. Immediately the seraph flies to Isaiah holding a live coal and touches the lips of Isaiah. The lips are not burned, but the uncleanness is seared away. As the seraph takes the live coal and presses it to Isaiah's mouth, his confessional cry is acknowledged. His guilt departs, and his sin is blotted out. (v. 7). The storyteller can enable the hearers to remember those incredible moments in life when wrongdoing is forgiven, when reconciliation occurs, or when one experiences the grace-filled moment when recognizing that, despite the past, one can indeed begin anew.

It is *after* Isaiah has experienced just such a wondrous moment, that he hears the voice of Yahweh (v. 8). The words are not directed to Isaiah—they seem to be directed to the community—to anyone and everyone who might be willing to listen to them—"Whom shall I send, and who will go for us?" Were there others who could have ventured forth to speak for Yahweh? Perhaps, but Isaiah has been made ready to go on a mission, even one yet undefined. And Isaiah responds, "Here am I; send me!" (v. 8 NRSV).

What is it that happens between the two outbursts of Isaiah? He first cries out, "Woe is me!" Later his cry is, "Here am I; send me!" What happens between is the remarkable transformation that one feels when one has experienced amazing grace.

As storytellers we prefer to end the story here. We tell stories with inspiring vignettes of courageous men and women who have, in their own lives, said "Here I am." That objective is worthy of our time and our attention. But to be true to the story of Isaiah we must continue and recount for those who listen the overwhelming challenge that Yahweh presented to Isaiah. We recount Isaiah's sadness as he heard the words Yahweh then spoke. "Keep listening, but do not comprehend; keep looking, but do not understand. Make the mind of this people dull, and stop their ears, and shut their eyes, so that they may not look with their eyes, and listen with their ears, and comprehend with their minds, and turn and be healed" (6:9-10 NRSV). Isaiah had been called to deliver a word that would not lead people toward life, but toward death. The words he was given to speak to the community were harsh words, words of confrontation about the emptiness and desolation in the land that Yahweh loved. To be true to the story of Isaiah we cannot end with the words "Here I am; send me!" ringing in our ears. We must hear the last words of Isaiah as he stands there frail but forgiven within the temple walls—"How long, O Lord?" Isaiah knows that the task for which he has been called will not be easy. Prophets are rarely called to speak the "easy" word. How long must he endure?

Retelling the Story

He worked a farm on the north edge of the City, preferring the old ways to the new. Not from nostalgia or stubbornness, but because the old ways had stood the test of time.

Most called him the Farmer. He had a name, a good name given him by a father and mother who worked the land before him. They named him George, but most called him the Farmer. Many

When Isaiah was called to be a prophet, God told him, "If you can stand the hostility and insults of my people then you will be my prophet. If you cannot bear their rage then tell me now and I will seek another prophet." You see, God already knew how a prophet who spoke the truth would be received. (*Sefer Ha-Aggadah* 477.82)

The sages said that when God spoke to prophets who were outside their faith the words they received were spoken in a kind of half speech, broken and truncated. When God spoke to the prophets of Israel, on the other hand, they received words that were whole, in a language that was loving and holy. That is why the seraphs that Isaiah saw were singing to God, "Holy, holy, holy is the Lord of Hosts." (*Genesis Rabbah* 52.4-5)

others farmed, but none like him. He farmed not merely to sustain his family or others, he farmed for the joy of it. He loved the earth and rain, sun and grain!

The Farmer had been considering the recent words of the Prophet. The Farmer listened to the Prophet, for when the Prophet spoke, the Farmer heard the echo of another Voice. It was the Voice he often heard in his own soul when he stopped talking in his prayers and listened. He knew this Voice. The ruler, the archon, of the City would pretend to listen to the Prophet, but he rarely did as the Prophet said he should. The Farmer worried about the City and the people who were lead by such a one as that.

He stood on the edge of his land and looked into the sky so blue it hurt to look at it. The Prophet had seen a vision when the old ruler had died. A glorious vision of angels and temple and heaven. But it was not the vision that cut to the heart of the Farmer, it was the calling of the One in the vision, the familiar sound of the Voice.

According to the rabbis, Isaiah received his first prophetic communication two years after Amos's prophesies stopped. On that same day, Uzziah claimed the privileges of the priesthood for himself. The king said he would have any priest killed who vocally opposed him. Uzziah, say the sages, even threatened the high priest, Azaria, when he attempted to stop the king from offering sacrifices at the altar. When the king attempted to offer the sacrifice, however, an earthquake began that caused a crack in the wall of the Temple. The sun shone through the crack striking Uzziah on the forehead. In that very spot, leprosy began to spread across the king's body. (Ginzberg, IV.262)

Who do I send? Who goes for me?

He was just a Farmer, but now what was going to happen? He had heard the words and now nothing would ever be the same. He claimed for himself no lineage of the Prophets. He never attended seminary or even the college. He was never one of the students who diligently followed the teachers from place to place—those who learned by the words of the teacher and even more by how their teacher lived.

No. He had worked the land, as his parents had before. He knew in his heart that he would always work the land, that his best destiny somehow revolved around the land.

But the words of the vision echoed throughout his waking and sleeping now.

Who do I send? Who goes for me?

What had the Prophet said? *Here am I! Send me.*

The farmer looked down from the sky and into the field where his destiny had always seemed to lie. And it still did, but something new was now here. Nothing would ever be the way it was before. Something was added, although it could not be seen or touched, and it was as real as the earth he plowed with iron.

Who do I send? Who goes for me?

The Farmer knew that Voice. It had called to him often.

What would the Farmer do now? *(R. Michael Sanders)*

The Shaking Heart and a Child of Hope

The prophet promises a child, Immanuel, who would be a sign of hope and who would drive away severe fear for a nation and its rulers who are under siege.

The Story

When it was reported to the house of David that the Aramaeans had made an alliance with the Ephraimites, king and people shook like forest trees shaking in the wind. The LORD said to Isaiah, 'Go out with your son Shear-jashub to meet Ahaz at the end of the conduit of the Upper Pool by the causeway leading to the Fuller's Field, and say to him: Remain calm and unafraid; do not let your nerve fail because of the blazing anger of Rezin with his Aramaeans and Remaliah's son, those two smouldering stumps of firewood. The Aramaeans with Ephraim and Remaliah's son have plotted against you: "Let us invade Judah and break her spirit," they said; "let us bring her over to our side, and set Tabeal's son on the throne." The Lord GOD has said:

This shall not happen now or ever,
that the rule in Aram should belong
    to Damascus,
the rule in Damascus to Rezin,
or that the rule in Ephraim should
    belong to Samaria,
and the rule in Samaria to
    Remaliah's son.

(Within sixty-five years a shattered
    Ephraim shall cease to be a
    nation.)
Have firm faith, or you will fail to
    stand firm.'

The LORD spoke further to Ahaz. 'Ask the LORD your God for a sign,' he said, 'whether from Sheol below or from heaven above.' But Ahaz replied: 'No, I will not put the LORD to the test by asking for a sign.' Then the prophet said: 'Listen, you house of David. Not content with wearing out the patience of men, must you also wear out the patience of my God? Because you do, the Lord of his own accord will give you a sign; it is this: A young woman is with child, and she will give birth to a son and call him Immanuel. By the time he has learnt to reject what is bad and choose what is good, he will be eating curds and honey; before that child has learnt to reject evil and choose good, the territories of those two kings before whom you now cringe in fear will lie desolate.

Comments on the Story

Ahaz was only twenty years old when he began to reign; perhaps that was not a young age for a man or woman in eighth-century Jerusalem. But for a person of *any* age the responsibility for the welfare of an entire nation is overwhelming. So it was for Ahaz who came to the throne of Judah and ruled for sixteen years.

While we know from the book of Isaiah that the prophet was sent with a word from Yahweh for this king, it is left to the editor of 2 Kings to fill in the details of the life of Ahaz. According to 2 Kings, some who came to the throne of Israel and Judah seemed to handle the pressures of "rulership" quite well—their priorities are kept straight and their allegiances with Yahweh are kept intact. Not so with Ahaz. During his reign he did *not* do what was right in the sight of Yahweh (2 Kings 16:2); he did not do as his ancestor David had done. The storyteller does not tell us why Ahaz became one of the most perverse rulers of Judah. It wasn't that he learned his perverse ways from his father. His father who had also ruled for sixteen years *had* done what was right in the sight of the Lord (15:34). But not Ahaz. Ahaz made offerings on the high places to other gods; these sacrifices he made everywhere—not only on high places, but also on the hills, and under every green tree (16:4). His unfaithfulnesses to Yahweh were not discreet, and one wonders if that caused confusion and concern among the people of Judah whom he ruled.

It was during this confusing time that King Rezin of Aram and King Pekah of Israel came mounting an attack on Jerusalem. Though they were not successful, the news that at least two nations had become allies against the nation of Judah brought terror into the hearts of Ahaz and his people. "The heart of Ahaz and the heart of his people shook as the trees of the forest shake before the wind" (Isa. 7:2 NRSV). This provocative image of fear captures the imagination of the storyteller. Ahaz is afraid. As the leader of the nation of Judah, as the protector of its welfare, Ahaz becomes frightened when he hears of the mounted attack made on the nation by two allied nations to the north. Two against one. His heart shook, and the hearts of the populace shook, as the branches and leaves of the tree shake in the wind.

Ahaz does not cry out. The people do not cry out to Yahweh, but Yahweh has heard their despair. Speaking through the prophet Isaiah who has just received his call, Yahweh sends a message of consolation. The forceful message of Yahweh comes in a four-fold imperative: "Take heed, be quiet, do not fear, and do not let your heart be faint" (v. 4 NRSV). The message of Yahweh is one of reassurance.

The storyteller can help her listeners remember times when they were as afraid as the people of Judah, times when the heart was shaking like trees in the wind. The storyteller can also remind her listeners of words of comfort received from well-meaning friends and family members, words like "don't be afraid" and "all will be well." Such was the word of Yahweh to Ahaz. The two countries of Aram and Israel, though they had plotted evil against Ahaz and the community, would not, Yahweh promised, stand. And thus the word to Judah was "do not be afraid." Isaiah recounts for Ahaz the "forecast" of the demise of the nations that now torment him. Isaiah warns Ahaz that if he does not stand firm in faith, he and the people of Judah will not stand firm at all (v. 9).

These words of comfort and challenge were not enough. Ahaz needed a sign, a visible sign that despite the seemingly imminent danger all will be well. Isaiah encourages Ahaz to ask for a sign from God, a sign of assurance. But Ahaz refuses, taking refuge in the excuse that it is not for humans to test God.

Isaiah offers to the reluctant Ahaz the sign for which he himself cannot ask. The sign given to Ahaz was this: "the young woman is with child and shall bear a son, and shall name him Immanuel. . . . " The sign of hope was to come through the life of a young woman.

Historians have held lengthy debate about the identity of the child. Was this a future king? A child of the prophet? Simply a child born to a Judean woman who will one day experience peace? Perhaps the question is an important one. Perhaps not. For the contemporary storyteller, the child can simply be a reminder that in a frightening and often confusing world there are visible signs of hope, signs that come from God, a God who is present with us. Immanuel! As we hear these words read during the Advent and Christmas seasons, it would be well for us to remember that those who first heard them were living in dangerous and confusing times. They were also afraid, their hearts shaking as trees in the wind.

Would this be enough for King Ahaz? Could he trust in this word? Would he keep faith in Yahweh, or would he, prompted by terror and motivated by a pervasive fear that would not dissipate, seek solace in the power of humankind—in a strong ally who perhaps could provide support and protection and ultimately peace?

Again the editor of 2 Kings provides us with the answer. Ahaz is not willing to rely on the spiritual to fight the threat of a foreign army. Ahaz sends messengers to the king of the mighty Assyrian empire saying, "I am your servant and your son. Come up, and rescue me from the hand of the king of Aram and from the hand of the king of Israel, who are attacking me" (16:7 NRSV).

As readers we are saddened by his choice. As storytellers we are encouraged to think of times in our own lives when fear prompted a desperate search to find something or someone in which to place hope. Fear can be so debilitating, so powerful, that it can cause us to place our confidences in the most unlikely of places. Ahaz was afraid, and though he was privy to the wise counsel of Isaiah, the prophet of Yahweh, he went searching for something much more tangible in which to place his trust—the might and the power of the Assyrian army.

We find it difficult to believe he could make such an unwise choice, and yet, when we are honest, we find that we also place our own hopes in the most hopeless of places. We often close our eyes to the signs of God's comforting and secure presence around us. The young woman gives birth to hope, and we do not see.

Retelling the Story

I remember I had finished my evening prayers and had just settled into bed when my father, Joshua, called, "Son, get up. I need you to come with me." So I pulled on my jeans and T-shirt and followed him, wondering, but asking no questions. While shivering in the autumn crispness we stood in the City's Central Park, by the footbridge. Then coming through the dusk, I saw who it was my father was waiting for: Kausak, the City's archon and his bodyguards approached running along the footpath, as they customarily did in the evening.

Kausak, surnamed Johnson, was descended from a long line of Johannine archons who had ruled the City, sometimes wisely and well, increasing both their family's fortunes and that of the City's first families. Even as a child Kausak had quickly grasped his position and learned from his father the art of maintaining his rule. Kausak had been so anxious to rule that for a few years before his father died, he and his father had even ruled together. For this reason the people gave him another name, "the Grasper." Kausak married Parthena, who although not well-born, was the daughter of a well-respected preacher. While the marriage had increased his popular support, Parthena, whose name means "maiden," had given him no children. Now in the fourteenth year of his reign, Kausak's distant cousin had obtained the financial backing of a rival

> The rabbi contended that God often employs small things for a divine purpose. Fleas, gnats, and other tiny creatures can inflict great misery. God chooses to do this to prove to the proud that their strength is an illusion. The sages said that God would use small things to correct the nations. Even the least things, and creatures in all creation are at God's disposal for the correction of all people. (*Numbers Rabbah* 18.22-23)

city, whose god was Baal. Through shrewd and ruthless financial dealing, the cousin had gained controlling interest in most of the Johnson family's and first families' corporate holdings, which were outside of the City. The cousin then relocated manufacturing plants from the City's outlying areas and transferred hundreds of workers' jobs. Many working-class families were separated because most had no choice but to follow their jobs. It seemed only a matter of time before the cousin would gain financial control of the City itself and replace the archon with his own oppressive choice.

Stepping boldly into the archon's path, my father did not wait to ask permission to speak but sternly said, "Pay attention. Keep calm, have no fear, do not let your heart sink because of your cousin and his backers who have plotted to ruin you. Yahweh says it shall not come true; it shall not be. Five or six years from now, your cousin's family and his backers will no longer be a people. But if you do not stand by Yahweh, you will not stand at all."

Then the archon's bodyguards tackled my father and me, pinning us down on the footpath. When they were satisfied that we were harmless, they let us stand, with our hands cuffed behind. But the Grasper said with some annoyance, "Let them go. Can't you see one is a man of God?" The Grasper turned away, dismissing us. It was obvious the Grasper did not believe the words my father spoke, but would not risk having it known he had insulted a man of God.

Undeterred, my father spoke to the archon a second time, "Ask Yahweh your God for a sign for yourself, either from heaven or hell." The Grasper instinctively called back a politically safe answer, "No, I will not put Yahweh to the test." My father responded without anger but with the power of words that were true. "Listen, Arcon, and the houses you represent, is it not enough to try my patience or will you try the patience of my God, too? Whether you ask or do not, Yahweh will give you a sign. The maiden is with child and she will give birth to a son whom she will call God-with-us. On curds and honey will he feed until he knows how to refuse evil and choose good. Before this child knows how to refuse evil and choose good the holdings of your cousin will become worthless and the Lord will bring times for you and your people and your father's house as have not come."

> Almost everything strong in creation can be bested by something else. Iron can split a stone mountain. Fire can melt iron, though. Water can put out fire. Clouds convey water across the sky. Wind can move clouds. The human body can withstand the strength of wind. Fear can overwhelm the human body, however. Wine can dissolve fear. Sleep can take away the effects of wine. Death, though, is stronger than any of these. (*Sefer Ha-Aggadah* 582.68)

The people were encouraged by this prophecy and wondered at the sign and when it would be fulfilled. Some looked for a greater fulfillment, others piled up stones by the City's gate. May the reader judge what I lived to see. At the celebration of the feast of the winter solstice, the archon announced the good news that Parthena expected a son. When the child was born, she named him Immanuel, but she called him David. As it turned out, the City itself was spared, and the people and the archon too. For a while, but not long, the Grasper followed the way of Yahweh. But as soon as the Grasper had a chance to outmaneuver his cousin by accepting the rites of Baal himself, he did. Shortly after, as a sign of his devotion to Baal, Kausak the Grasper made his son David pass through the fire. But the boy did not die. *(R. Michael Sanders)*

Before and After

A marvelous ruler will come and bring hope to a people who languish in a desparate darkness.

The Story

For there is no escape for an oppressed people.

Formerly the lands of Zebulun and Naphtali were lightly regarded, but afterwards honour was bestowed on Galilee of the Nations on the road beyond Jordan to the sea.

The people that walked in darkness
have seen a great light;
on those who lived in a land as dark
as death
a light has dawned.
You have increased their joy
and given them great gladness;
they rejoice in your presence
as those who rejoice at harvest,
as warriors exult when dividing
spoil.

For you have broken the yoke that
burdened them,
the rod laid on their shoulders,
the driver's goad, as on the day of
Midian's defeat.

The boots of earth-shaking armies on
the march,
the soldiers' cloaks rolled in blood,
all are destined to be burnt, food
for the fire.

For a child has been born to us, a
son is given to us;
he will bear the symbol of dominion
on his shoulder,
and his title will be:
Wonderful Counsellor, Mighty Hero,
Eternal Father, Prince of Peace.
Wide will be the dominion
and boundless the peace
bestowed on David's throne and on
his kingdom,
to establish and support it
with justice and righteousness
from now on, for evermore.
The zeal of the LORD of Hosts will
do this.

Comments on the Story

Contrast is one of the remarkable tools of the storyteller's trade. Many a tale has been spun with a phrase such as, "this is how things were," *but* "this is how things are now." Or, "this is how things are now," *but* "this is how they will be later." The contrast in Isaiah 9:1-7 is sharp; the text provides rich imagery that describes the current plight of the Judean people and the coming transformation that God's people will experience, the "now" and the "later."

Chapter 8:11-22 of the NRSV recounts the words Yahweh spoke to Isaiah while Yahweh's hand was strong upon him. Yahweh warns the prophet not to walk in the way of the wayward people. Isaiah is called not to fear what others fear, but to fear only Yahweh. Isaiah is called not to be in dread of what others dread, but to dread only Yahweh. Poetically, the text describes the plight of Yahweh's people who do not "wait," nor do they place their hope (v. 17) in their God. Darkness becomes the formative metaphor used to describe the experience of the wayward ones. They will experience no dawn (v. 20). They will be greatly distressed and hungry (v. 21). They will look everywhere, but they will see only distress and darkness, gloom and anguish. Isaiah cannot emphasize the formative metaphor strongly enough! Again, he says, they will be thrust into thick darkness (v. 22).

The storyteller will have no difficulty describing the plight of a person, of a people who have no light. With no dawn there is no new beginning. Without the possibility of beginning again, there can be no hope. Darkness brings gloom and despair. A people walking in darkness walk with hesitancy and with fear. Directionless, they grope into nothingness, seeking for the slightest touch of something familiar, something that will lend perspective and help them along the way.

Those who are walking in darkness will see a great light. With this metaphor of God's saving action our text begins; it contrasts the disastrous fate of Israel at the hands of the foreign enemy with the salvation that is to come. Isaiah *names* the darknesses that will be no more—burden . . . [with oppression] . . . tramping warriors . . . garments rolled in blood (vv. 4-5). In the midst of the darkness the people will see light. In the land of deep darkness, light shines (v. 2). Words can barely express the joyful response of the multitudes. Their joy is increased, they rejoice like the rejoicing at the most magnificent of harvests. And then, like the best of stories where we experience the celebration before we know that which is being celebrated, finally the light is named. The hope, the light, is to come through a child. A child will be born, Isaiah tells the community, "for us." The son is given, Isaiah tells the community, "to us." This ruler to come is called:

> Wonderful Counselor (a wise political guide and leader);
> Mighty God (a strong warrior, one who can defeat the enemy);
> Everlasting Father (one who is beneficent, who has concern for the welfare of the people); and
> Prince of Peace (one who will bring wholeness and harmony). [Isa. 9:6 NRSV]

This possible coronation liturgy contains all of the affirmations one would expect on such an occasion—there is rejoicing over the hopes that the community places in the new one who has come to rule. There is confidence that this person and the community will be blessed by God. There is faith that the one coming to the throne will usher in the new age. While the issues surrounding the determination of the historical setting of the oracle remain complex, and while this text could have been recited at the accession of Hezekiah or even Josiah to the throne, it is placed in Isaiah to offer to a struggling community a word of hope.

The contemporary storyteller is challenged to discover fresh examples of new beginnings. What is the darkness in which individuals, the community, and our world live? It will become the responsibility of the storyteller *to name* those darknesses so that the community will realize their need for light. It will be more difficult for the storyteller *to name* the light that will break through our darkness. The description of the light will have to be so compelling that it will break through our apathy and our cynicism and cause us to ask ourselves anew—Is there a light that can penetrate our darkness? Do we believe that a piercing light can shine in and redeem us?

According to Isaiah, salvation can come. Isaiah maintains that this will happen because of the "zeal" of Yahweh. What appears to be beyond possibility can be certain. Yahweh, through Yahweh's passion and fury, with a great sense of urgency will see that the light will come. Isaiah believes this to be true. Do we? The storyteller can enable us to find our own answers to that very important question.

Retelling the Story

The words of the Prophet ended, echoing on slightly longer down the streets of the City. But they would echo longer in the hearts of some who heard. The crowd slowly went their way. Some went to talk more about what they had heard. Others forgot almost as soon as the words stopped echoing down the canyon. It was as if one of the falcons that nested on the ledges of the high-rises had swooped down and snatched the words from the very air!

But not the Farmer. He listened and remembered so he could tell others what he heard.

The Prophet said that all the troubles of the City, the darkness of ancient hurts and present fears would come to an end. But the end was not to be

Even at night there are the moon and stars to offer some light. The darkest time of the night is just before dawn. The moon, stars, and planets have all set by then. The rabbis said that this was the deepest darkness that humans could know. Yet, it is at this darkest time of the night that God offers the gift of the dawn to the world. The people who waited in darkness then see a great light. Each day is, therefore, a testimony to God's faithfulness. (*Sefer Ha-Aggadah* 761.18)

53

brought about by a military solution. The City's well-trained army, which was outfitted with the latest and most expensive weapons in order to frighten and subdue the City's weaker neighbors, was not the answer. The conquest of other cities that would end their economic boycotts of the City's goods was not the answer, nor was the acquiring of more rich land.

The answer was not in the economic reform touted by opponents of the government.

The answer was not fewer or more taxes.

No. The answer lay with the birth of a child. A special child, one who would embody the very being of God. What could all this mean? How could this be? Words like "Wonderful Councillor," "Mighty God," "Everlasting Father," and the strangest of all "Prince of Peace"? Peace? How could there be peace when all their hearts were filled with fear and want and envy?

> One of the rabbis said that the people waiting in darkness are like those who stop attending the house of prayer. There was one qualification, though. If people miss prayer services for a godly reason they still walk in the light. If they miss for any other reason they remain in darkness. (*Sefer Ha-Aggadah* 530.230)

And how could a child ever be the answer? How could a baby bring justice and peace? When had a child ever done this?

This caused the Farmer to remember the birth of his daughter. How he held her and kissed her. How he held the warmness of her close and felt the warmness all the way through into his heart. He again experienced the incredible feelings he had for her. He remembered now the vow he made to his God that day. He would never let his child be hungry or wounded or mocked or ever left alone. He remembered the other thousand promises a father or mother would make.

> Other rabbis said that those Isaiah referred to as waiting in darkness are the poor, especially those who have to depend on others to give them food, if they are to have anything to eat. Those who have to wander the world begging for a crust of bread are those for whom the promise is made that upon them light will shine. In other words everyone will have enough to eat. (*Sefer Ha-Aggadah* 600.287)

What if part of the answer was in the nature of a baby and how easily all loved a child? Surely this was not all of the answer. Certainly this was not all that the Prophecy had intimated. But what if part of the answer for a broken City and a broken world resided in the love that all good parents feel for their child? What if all fathers and mothers began to feel for all the other children in the world as they felt for their own? Was not this a taste, a preview, of what

God felt for God's children? And would not the best symbol of this be a child? Perhaps even God's own child?

What if there were a special festival inaugurated to celebrate this? A new holiday emphasizing the birth of such a special child? Yes, the Farmer could see it in his mind now. For that brief moment all could feel and know this love. And maybe, one by one, begin to see all children (and are we all not someone's child?) with this love.

How wise God was, after all! *(R. Michael Sanders)*

To Catch the Vision

*A leader will emerge who is so righteous and just, so able to subdue the
wicked, that all creatures would dwell without conflict, death, or pain.*

The Story

Then a branch will grow from
    the stock of Jesse,
and a shoot will spring from his
    roots.
On him the spirit of the LORD will
    rest:
a spirit of wisdom and
    understanding,
a spirit of counsel and power,
a spirit of knowledge and fear of the
    LORD;
and in the fear of the LORD will be his
    delight.
He will not judge by outward
    appearances
or decide a case on hearsay;
but with justice he will judge the
    poor
and defend the humble in the land
    with equity;
like a rod his verdict will strike the
    ruthless,
and with his word he will slay the
    wicked.
He will wear the belt of justice,
and truth will be his girdle.

Then the wolf will live with the lamb,
and the leopard lie down with the
    kid;
the calf and the young lion will feed
    together,
with a little child to tend them.
The cow and the bear will be friends,
and their young will lie down
    together;
and the lion will eat straw like cattle.
The infant will play over the cobra's
    hole,
and the young child dance over the
    viper's nest.
There will be neither hurt nor harm
    in all my holy mountain;
for the land will be filled with the
    knowledge of the LORD,
as the waters cover the sea.

On that day a scion from the root of
    Jesse
will arise like a standard to rally the
    peoples;
the nations will resort to him,
and his abode will be glorious.

Comments on the Story

The first ten chapters of Isaiah are punctuated with heavy, sobering words
from Yahweh to the people of Judah. The accusations Yahweh brings to the
community and Yahweh's feelings of despair at the unfaithfulness of the
covenanted people form a seemingly endless tirade of reprimands and admoni-

tions. As chapter 11 begins, the reader finds that Judah is now only a "stump." The metaphor of the tree is used to depict what remains—a stump with roots. The stump appears to be dead, but it is not. As the text continues, the editor of Isaiah "lifts the eyes" of the readers to a higher plane. Suddenly and without warning, the tirade comes to an abrupt end, and the reader finds juxtaposed to harsh words of reproach and derision, a new word—a vision—an acknowledgment that life is about to be different! There is an intrusion of good news, very good news, to the people of Judah. A shoot will come from the stump of Jesse and a branch will grow from the roots (v. 1). The reader is alerted that what will follow is a word of hope.

Isaiah 11:1-10 is one of those surprising pieces of literature that leaps off the page and takes the reader by surprise. This unit in Isaiah, along with 7:10-17 and 9:1-7, forms a trio of passages that describes and announces the leader to come. The character of the king is described in verses 2-5 in great detail. The spirit of Yahweh will rest upon this special one; three pairs of gifts will be his, made manifest by the spirit of Yahweh. This one to come will have:

> the spirit of wisdom and understanding,
> the spirit of counsel and might,
> the spirit of knowledge and fear of Yahweh (v. 2 based on NRSV).

The text continues by describing what this new king will do. The king will judge with righteousness and decide with equity (v. 4). This text describes a ruler with a single-minded devotion to the community and to justice, a devotion that necessitates an abandonment of one's own ambition. With this leadership the order of the earth will be reestablished and there will be peace. This is not a peace simply among humans, it is a peace that affects all of creation. Harmony among all of God's creations will be restored.

The images of this age to come (described in vv. 6-10) are a veritable treasure chest for the storyteller. They have been captured by poets and painters for generations. The wolf shall live with the lamb, the leopard will lie down with the kid, the calf and the lion will peacefully coexist, and the cow and the bear will graze together. The nursing child plays over the asp and the weaned child over the home of the poisonous snake. It is a picture of a world where no one "hurts or destroys," and where the most vulnerable among us are safe.

The storyteller asks—What would this violent world be like, if no one hurt or destroyed another? What unlikely groups of persons would finally be able to dwell with one another? And perhaps most captivating, What would it be like if the world's children lived in safety? Is that not a vision we could share?

The child starving in Somalia, rib cage protruding through sun baked skin.

The child who cannot play unsupervised in her front yard because the frequency of gunfire or the fear of roving predators makes her home an unsafe place.

The child who does not know if he will make it through another day without bruises on his skin from a frustrated parent who finds the pressures of living in an unjust and unkind world too much to bear.

The child who cowers in the corner of her bedroom not knowing that molestation is not a part of every child's life.

The child in a war torn country, torn from the loving arms of a parent, or sent away by a mother who hopes and prays that somewhere else, the child may find a better life.

What if all the children of the world had a song to sing? Or could walk safely and comfortably through the field, could play anywhere—and no viper would harm him or her?

What if, for all the children of the world, nightmares were not the daily reality?

What a dream! What a vision—where children are safe and where the most likely of enemies live life beside one another, where none will be hurt or destroyed because the whole earth will be filled with the knowledge of Yahweh.

By placing this vision of the day to come in the midst of the description of the stark realities of life, the editor of First Isaiah in a subtle but shocking way, reminds us that occasionally we need to stop and allow ourselves the wonderful privilege of seeing life, not how it is, but how it can be. Ironically, then, this text functions like a good story. In seeing how the world can be, we are sadly reminded how it now is. We long for a better place.

Retelling the Story

"Tell me how it will be again, Joshua." I can still hear the little boy's request, and see my father, Joshua, rest a scarred hand, like the missing piece of a puzzle, upon the boy's face. It had rested there before, on a day when the rites of Baal demanded a sacrifice.

On that pitiless day Kausak, the archon of the City, had taken up his new office as Khanna-Baal, priest of Baal. Kausak intended to offer his infant son, David, as a burned sacrifice to his newfound god. The procession had arrived at the temple, and the City's first families were there too with their small sacrifices. The fire had been kindled and Baal's bronze arms were stretched over it. To the side a small coffin waited, adorned with figures of a weeping Kausak and his wife Parthena.

At the signal, drums rolling to mask the cries, Kausak, Khanna-Baal let his son slip from his grasp down the bronze arms and into the fire. But in an instant my father, Joshua, slid his hand under a side of the infant's head and grabbing a leg, snatched the infant from the fire, smothering the flaming horror against his body and cloak. Parthena stepped between Kausak and my father and said, "My lord Khanna-Baal, this child is not your sacrifice. Your son died when he was born and on that day I purchased a child to take his place. Do not harm the man of God, and do not bother with this worthless child." Whether Parthena told the truth or lied no one could tell. Even if he lived, his burns would prevent anyone from seeing who the child resembled, and Kausak could not risk making a worthless sacrifice. The families parted to the right and to the left to let the man of God, my father, pass on. Some followed him from that place. But most stayed.

After this Kausak divorced Parthena, who went back with her dowry to her father's house. She made no inquiries after the child she called David. For this reason it is idly told that Parthena and Kausak's son, Immanuel, did not really die at birth, but rather than see him burn, Parthena left her son in the marketplace to be found by traders. People speculated the child was likely sold abroad. It is just as reasonable to think she had nothing to do with David because her interest would place him in danger. But perhaps the explanation is simpler: Parthena was overcome by shame.

Whether Parthena knew it or not, David did live, even thrived, though he was horribly scarred. My father's hands healed, too, with scars that matched David's. They had passed through the

> Isaiah said that "the land will be filled with the knowledge of God, as the waters cover the sea." The rabbis unpacked this poetic image this way: The knowledge of God was like a drink of water to a thirsty soul. Like water, it ran downhill from a proud student to a humble one. Just as water keeps better in clay jars than in silver carafes, so the knowledge of God resides well in a student who is willing to become a clay jar. Just as an important person will ask a humble one for a drink of water, so a great scholar must be willing to learn from even a rank beginner. The rabbis offer a word of warning, though, saying that water can drown one who cannot swim, and the inexperienced can be overwhelmed and swept away by the knowledge of God. There is at least one way that the knowledge of God is not like water: Water may quench the thirst but it does not make the heart glad as wine does. In that way the knowledge of God is more like wine than water.
> (*Song of Songs Rabbah* 1.2[3])

fire together and would not be parted. Sheltered in my father's house, David's bedtime ritual always asked, "Tell me how it will be again, Joshua, how the little boy will lead them." And my father never tired of telling how someday there would be no hurt, no harm, on all Yahweh's holy mountain, because the country will be filled with the knowledge of Yahweh as the waters swell the sea. Then the wolf will live with the lamb, the panther will lie down with the kid. The cow and the bear will make friends, and their young will lie down together. The lion will eat straw like an ox then. And the lion's cub and a calf will feed together with a little boy to lead them. At this point little David would often ask if he could be the boy to lead the cub and the calf. "Perhaps. God knows," my father would answer. What could my father say? He told David this story of changing nature, because he did not have the heart to dwell on the nature of the human heart, and he could find no words to explain to David the reason for his burns.

As David grew older Joshua would add that Yahweh promised a righteous faithful judge would come, on whom the very spirit of Yahweh would rest with wisdom and insight, counsel and power, and knowledge. This judge will not judge by appearances, give no verdict on hearsay, but judge the wretched with integrity giving equity to the poor, striking the ruthless and sentencing the wicked to death. My father knew that the people would judge David by his appearance and thinking him wretched would look away, sentencing him to invisibility.

But David was not wretched. He grew to be a man with eyes fixed on the holy mountain of Yahweh on which there is no hurt. With his compassion he gentled the natures of many. Who can say if he did not lead some to Yahweh? Kausak however, was never gentled and his nature never changed. He married again, and at times the ambitions of both Baal and Kausak fed together on Kausak's offspring. *(R. Michael Sanders)*

I Will Give Thanks

In spite of devastating judgment that the prophet has witnessed and invoked, a person and a people burst forth in a rousing song about the Lord's salvation.

The Story

On that day you will say:
'I shall praise you, LORD.
Though you were angry with me,
your anger has abated,
and you have comforted me.
God is my deliverer.
I am confident and unafraid,
for the LORD is my refuge and defence
and has shown himself my deliverer.'

With joy you will all draw water
from the wells of deliverance.
On that day you will say:

'Give thanks to the LORD, invoke him
    by name,
make known among the peoples
    what he has done,
proclaim that his name is exalted.
Sing psalms to the LORD, for he has
    triumphed;
let this be known in all the world.
Cry out, shout aloud, you dwellers in
    Zion,
for the Holy One of Israel is among
    you in majesty.'

Comments on the Story

Frequently in studies on First Isaiah, Chapter 12 goes virtually ignored. Perhaps because of its hymnic character and its designation as a late addition to the book, its message and function have typically been assumed to add little to our understanding of the book of Isaiah. This joyful song that brings closure to the first eleven chapters of Isaiah, however, begs the storyteller to ask, What is it that would cause an individual or a community to burst out spontaneously into song? What causes great rejoicing? For what are we thankful?

They look deceptively similar, the two songs (vv. 1-2, 3-6) found in the twelfth chapter of Isaiah. Thematically both songs strike the same chord of thanksgiving (vv. 1 and 3), and the worshiper is overwhelmed with gratitude. But on closer inspection, the words are found to give expression to different life experiences—the first song (which uses singular verb forms) is the heartfelt thanksgiving of the individual worshiper; the second, a congregational hymn (which uses plural, imperative verb forms), is the heartfelt thanksgiving of the community. We must look closer to see what has put gratitude into the hearts and the mouths of those who worship.

For the individual worshiper (vv. 1-2), the heart is filled with thanksgiving for an experience of forgiveness and of grace. The person perceiving that God has been angry, finds that now God provides a comforting presence (v. 1).

The song reinforces the idea inherent in Isaiah's name itself—"Yahweh is salvation." One who experiences salvation is trusting and will not be afraid. God indeed has become salvation itself. Moreover, this first song in 12:1-2 focuses on the feelings that salvation brings to the one who is saved by God— feelings of comfort, trust, courage, and strength.

The second song begins with the picture of the joyful worshiper drawing water from the "wells of salvation" (v. 3 NRSV). This metaphor reinforces for the reader the idea of the abundant presence of God, a presence that continues to pour forth good things. In contrast to the first song, the second is composed of a string of imperatives outlining what the worshipers will/should do in response to the salvation that God has rendered—give thanks, call on God's name, make known the deeds, proclaim, sing praises, shout and sing. Thematically the two songs are tied to one another. They are songs of thanksgiving and of joy, and they are both songs that are born from the experience of salvation. But the differences between the two songs—their individual and communal natures, and the different foci of internal feeling (vv. 1-2) and external response (vv. 3-6)—call forth different stories.

These hymns were most likely used in worship. In Isaiah, however, the song and the hymn are not recorded simply to render an account of what people sang during worship in the eighth century B.C.E., or as a basis for what we might sing today. The two hymns function as assurances that announce salvation, to make emphatic the assertion that the salvation predicted in the eleven chapters of Isaiah will indeed come to pass.

The first eleven chapters of Isaiah are filled with words of both hope and despair, judgment and forgiveness. Chapter 12 stands in relation to the negative images of judgment and destruction like those seen in Isaiah 1, 3, 5, and 6. Here the rebellious are devoured by the sword, daughter Zion is smitten with scabs, Yahweh's vineyard is made a waste, the cities lie waste without inhabitant, houses are without men and the land is utterly desolate. To those images chapter 12 says that the anger of Yahweh is turned away and Yahweh will comfort the people.

To the positive proclamations of salvation like those found in Isaiah 2, 4, 9, and 11, chapter 12 also responds. In those chapters the mountain of the Lord will be established, the branch of the Lord will again be beautiful and glorious, people who have walked in darkness will see a great light, and the remnant will be brought back as the Israelites were brought back from the land of Egypt. To these words of assurance, Isaiah 12 says "Yes!" Those things will come to pass, and Yahweh's people will sing praises for all that Yahweh has done. The Holy One of Israel is in their midst.

The storyteller, then, is called upon to think of times when men and women have found the courage and the hope to sing and proclaim salvation and deliverance when the eyes see little sign of deliverance on the earth's landscape. The storyteller is invited to think about songs of endurance, ballads of faithfulness and certainty that have been sung in the face of disaster and hopelessness.

The storyteller is then challenged to tell a tale that will call forth from the listeners a spontaneous and rousing doxology of praise.

Retelling the Story

The preacher was staring out the window of the prison waiting to see the condemned man. He remembered seeing a miracle once in another prison, long ago in a strange land called Indiana. Some thought the place was a legend. Others thought it was a remnant of lost memory or perhaps a vision of what was to come.

The preacher clearly remembered the judge who presided over the trial in Indiana. A very bad man came and stood before the judge. There was no doubt about the man's guilt. This man named Jim drew the fullest penalty of the law. For his horrendous crime he was convicted, and the judge sentenced him to death.

The judge was a good man, a God-fearer. He often was seen at the great worship assemblies. It grieved him to sentence Jim to death, but his grief was more for those who suffered under the pitiless hurt of this man. And the law was quite specific in the case and gave the judge little discretion.

It was the preacher's ministry to visit prisons; that was the reason he ended up in that legendary place called Indiana. The preacher gathered a group of believers who were willing to volunteer and go to that prison to bring some comfort and hope to those in prison. He knew Jim was waiting in that prison in the terrible place called "death row." The preacher had corresponded with

> One rabbi compares the gratitude expressed in the first verses of this passage to a merchant who set out on a journey with a competitor. The competitor made it to the ship, but the merchant happened to get a pretty nasty thorn in his foot that delayed him so that he missed the same ship. Thinking the delay had cost him business, the merchant began to curse his bad fortune. Some time later, though, word came that the ship on which the competitor had sailed had encountered a storm and had sunk. Then the merchant fell down on his knees to thank God that his bad fortune had suddenly turned into good fortune, in that his life had been spared. He prayed, "I shall praise you, Lord. Though you are angry with me, your anger has abated, and you have comforted me." (*Sefer Ha-Aggadah* 511.62)

him and believed that something had changed in the man. Somehow the judge heard of their intended visit and asked if he might go also. The preacher was a little surprised, but readily agreed.

The warden escorted the group through the prison. One in the group sang while the rest ministered in other ways. The preacher was amazed at the radiance and joy he witnessed in Jim.

The time came for them to leave. The preacher was surprised to see the judge in Jim's cell talking. He waited as long as he could, but he had to go other places, to see other folks. He made noises about it being late, but the judge tarried in the cell with the condemned man. Finally the preacher called out, "I'm sorry, but we really must go."

Even some of the greatest of their ancestors were not above criticism, according to the sages. Hezekiah, who was generally considered to be an upstanding man and leader, was said to have a heart that was "puffed up." This was said of him because he and his soldiers were too proud or unconcerned to sing a song of praise to God. When Isaiah told Hezekiah's troops to "Sing psalms to the Lord," they asked, "Why?" Isaiah explained, "Because the Lord has triumphed, let that be known throughout the world." To this the troops replied, "Oh, everybody already knows that."

When the prophet brought this matter before the king, Hezekiah is reputed to have said, "My study of Torah makes up for any songs that my army and I do not sing." This refusal to rejoice in what God had done is the reason that Hezekiah is spoken of as being "puffed up." (*Sefer Ha-Aggadah* 138.163)

"You don't understand," the judge called back. "I am the man who sentenced him to die. Now I see that he has changed, that God has changed him. He is my brother, and we must pray together."

It was a moment when time stood still and the angels held their breath before bursting out with joy and praise. The judge, unable to change what had happened or what would happen, was praying with the man he had condemned to death. And the condemned man was smiling and praying, for all intents and purposes, with his executioner. There they stood, holding the Holy Book in their hands, talking, smiling, praying for each other. Surely the one should have looked down on the other! Surely the prisoner should despise the judge! But, no. The love was real. The forgiveness was a physical thing the preacher wished he could snatch out of the air and show to the doubters he knew he would encounter on other days.

The preacher turned from the window and his thoughts. So impossible in human terms, but something so real with the power of the One God.

Could it happen for Paul? (*R. Michael Sanders*)

Old, Faithful, Sure

Some day soon, God's weary people will find a place to rest, to obtain comfort.

The Story

LORD, you are my God;
I shall exalt you, I shall praise
your name,
for you have done wonderful
things,
long-planned, certain and sure.
You have turned cities into heaps of
ruin,
fortified towns into rubble;
every mansion in the cities is swept
away,
never to be rebuilt.
For this many a cruel nation holds
you in honour,
the cities of ruthless peoples treat you
with awe.
Truly you have been a refuge to the
poor,
a refuge to the needy in their
distress,
shelter from tempest, shade from
heat.
For the blast of the ruthless is like an
icy storm
or a scorching drought;
you subdue the roar of the foe,
and the song of the ruthless dies
away.

On this mountain the LORD of Hosts
will prepare
a banquet of rich fare for all the
peoples,
a banquet of wines well matured,
richest fare and well-matured wines
strained clear.
On this mountain the LORD will
destroy
that veil shrouding all the peoples,
the pall thrown over all the nations.
He will destroy death for ever.
Then the Lord GOD will wipe away
the tears
from every face,
and throughout the world
remove the indignities from his
people.
The LORD has spoken.

On that day the people will say:
'See, this is our God;
we have waited for him and he will
deliver us.
This is the LORD for whom we have
waited;
let us rejoice and exult in his
deliverance.'

For the hand of the LORD will rest on
this mountain,
but Moab will be trampled where he
stands,
as straw is trampled in the slush of a
midden.

Comments on the Story

Following the oracles against the nations, found in Isaiah 13–23, are four chapters which are often titled the "Isaiah Apocalypse." Chapters 24–27, which compose the apocalypse, are the subject of rich and varied debates: their provenance, the determination of the chapters' authorship and dates of creation, and the relationship between these chapters and their literary context remain uncertain. Regardless of the solution to these scholarly questions, the chapters describe a destruction in poetic and mythical language. There are images of universal devastation and words that describe the deliverance that follows. There are oracles of doom as well as victory songs. The storyteller will want to read the section in its entirety to avail herself of the rich imagery and the metaphoric wonders that the author uses to describe what will happen "on that day" which is to come.

Out of the entire sequence, only verses from chapter 25 are part of the lectionary cycle. The verses are significant, however, for they are read in most of our churches during Pentecost, or on Easter evening, either every year, or as alternative readings for Easter (Year B) and on All Saints Day (Year B). Moreover, the lectionary officials have graciously omitted the ending of Isaiah 25, which recounts for the reader an oracle of doom against Moab. While it is true that many of the best sermons or story plots come from the texts found *between* the lections, we will focus here on verses 1-10*a*, which are rich with possibility for the storyteller.

The first ten verses of chapter 25 can themselves be divided into two units. The first is a song, similar to the songs of the psalter that speak a word of thanksgiving to God. The imagery of the song provokes in the hearer images of rest and of comfort. Yahweh, the psalmist's God, has historically done wonderful things for God's people. This is a God who can be trusted—who has plans formed of old, faithful and sure (v. 1). The storyteller is given the opportunity to re-present for the hearer images of trust and confidence that bring comfort—images of those persons, perhaps places or things, that bring visions of faithfulness and surety. While the psalm of thanksgiving in verses 1-5 is dotted with reminders of desolate cities and the destruction of the ruthless (a reversal of the status quo), the images of comfort and safety prevail. Yahweh is like a refuge to the poor and needy, the shelter from the rainstorm, the shade from the heat—each metaphor a seed from which a story can grow.

This outburst of thanksgiving is followed (in vv. 6-10*a*) by a description of the wonderful day to come. The terse images provide for the storyteller an assortment of rich and poignant pictures of what will be. The vision in 25:6-10 takes place, as do other visions in Isaiah, on a high mountain. Here, on the mountain, Yahweh will make for *all* peoples a great banquet (a significant mythological symbol in many cultures that lead a hand-to-mouth existence)—a feast rich with food and wines. This will be a wonderful place where the death that has formerly swallowed women and men will now itself be swallowed. Tears will be wiped away from faces; disgrace will be taken away from all the earth (v. 8). The people will be aware of the presence of Yahweh who has provided the feast and the relief for them. It is in the last refrain (v. 9) that we become aware that this wonderful confirmation of God's presence and care is not unanticipated. The people have *waited* for God to save them. Again in verse 9 it is emphasized that the one who has come is Yahweh for whom the people have *waited*. They will be glad and rejoice.

The idea of "waiting" for Yahweh is a common thematic element in the psalter. The psalmist often sings about his waiting for Yahweh to come and to save.

"Do not let those who wait for you be put to shame . . . " (Ps. 25:3 NRSV).

" . . . but those who wait for the LORD shall inherit the land" (Ps. 37:9 NRSV).

" . . . for you I wait all day long" (Ps. 25:5 NRSV).

"May integrity and uprightness preserve me, for I wait for you" (Ps. 25:21 NRSV).

This Hebrew word for "wait" is sometimes translated "hope" and sometimes "expect." It is with expectation that the people of Yahweh have waited for this day when salvation would come to the peoples.

The people wait for Yahweh, and they will not be disappointed. The story ends in a note of confident assurance, and therefore, one of comfort. The people have waited for Yahweh that they might be saved. This joyful confirmation of the people's hope and expectation brings to the reader of Isaiah an ironic twist, a sad reality that cannot be shaken. In the song of the vineyard (Isaiah 5), Yahweh also waits expectantly. Yahweh *waits* for the field to yield good grapes (5:2). Yahweh *waits* hopefully and expectantly for justice, but looking upon the world sees only bloodshed. Yahweh *waits* for righteousness, but hears only cries. Yahweh waits. Yahweh is disappointed. The people who wait for Yahweh, however, are never disappointed. Their confidence has not been misplaced.

Retelling the Story

From the summit of the hill I can see the City stretched below, gleaming this

> Someday God will gather the righteous in the Garden of Eden, say the sages. God will be in the middle and the righteous will gather in a circle around the divine presence and point toward the Holy One saying, in the words of Isaiah, "See, this is our God; we have waited for him and he will deliver us. This is the Lord for whom we have waited; let us rejoice and exult in his deliverance." (*Sefer Ha-Aggadah* 401.17)

spring day, except for the bare brown scar where the temple of Baal once stood on the acropolis. No one goes near that polluted place, not to build or to plant. Scraped bare, the place was sown with salt so that the ground itself could exhibit its shame. The residence of Kausak, that pitiless archon of the City, sits beside the scar, now a pile of rubble upon which the City's mothers throw their garbage. Death ended Kausak's songs to Baal, and the sacrifice of children in Baal's fires. They will never be rebuilt, that temple, that residence, those fires. I am satisfied with the ruin.

Why am I permitted to see it? I should be like Kausak, dead and not honored, not buried with his fathers but disposed of like the carcass of an animal. I, Parthena, Kausak's former wife, should be like the rubble covered with the City's garbage. I alone let Kausak take the infant. I alone let Kausak place him on the arms of Baal. I did not move as the infant rolled helplessly into the fire. It was the man of God who snatched him out of the flames, not I. I will not call myself his mother. What mother, what woman could do what I did?

David, the infant I was willing to see die, has for all his life exhibited the fire's brand, but I have hidden my shame these forty years within the walls of my father's house. Today I mean to exhibit my shame on this hill, in this place before the people against whom I have sinned. If the hand of Yahweh spares me, it will be well; if other hands find stones to throw, it will be very well. I am an old woman who knows the truth: I have long deserved to die.

As I cross over the hill's summit, the City disappears. Now I can see the people seated on the hillside's natural amphitheater. The prophet is already speaking. His name is Paul, a compelling, passionate man from the farmland around the City. "On Yahweh's holy mountain He will remove the mourning veil that covers all nations, " Paul is saying. "He will destroy death. He will wipe away the tears from every cheek and will take away his people's shame everywhere on the earth."

I continue to walk down the stone steps feeling a shocked stillness growing behind me until both I and the stillness reach the floor of the amphitheater. I do not dare look up but I can speak the truth. "I am Parthena. I have sinned greatly against Yahweh and against you."

Because I was looking down, I was unsure whose hands had, almost roughly, pulled off my veil. I had expected to be mocked first, and then condemned. Instead I heard a voice saying, "You are dead no longer in the tomb of your father's house, but alive again, Parthena." Looking up I saw it was that same David who wiped away my tears, who with his forgiveness took away my shame. This was the work of Yahweh my God, in whom I had hoped for salvation. Yahweh my God has certainly carried out his excellent design, long-planned, trustworthy, and true. He has set a feast for us on this hillside and called us all to rejoice in his salvation. *(R. Michael Sanders)*

The children of Israel might be compared to the bride of a king. When they were married, the king wrote out what today we would call a prenuptial agreement. He gave her beautiful clothes in royal purple, a number of apartments, and towns in his kingdom over which she exercised care. Then the king went away on a long journey. The weeks turned into months, the months turned into years, and still he did not return. The queen's companions told her that the king must be dead or had deserted her for another. Even so she would not give up hope. When she was about to despair she would remember the agreement he had made with her and this would comfort her. Finally, the king returned from his journey and her hope was vindicated. The king told her, "I am amazed that you were able to wait for me." She told him, "My companions attempted to convince me that you were gone forever, but your promises to me encouraged me to keep faith though you were gone many years."

Just so the nations mocked Israel's faith in the God who called them out and claimed them. They said, "Look at how you have suffered. Where is your God? Surely your God has deserted you. How long are you going to suffer for the sake of one who is gone?" But Israel was able to keep faith because of the promises of God to them. And finally they, too, were vindicated. God said to them, "I am amazed that you were able to wait so long." (*Sefer Ha-Aggadah* 387.2)

The Wilderness Way

Zion is restored, and the people throng the highways in return to the florid land.

The Story

Let the wilderness and the
    parched land be glad,
let the desert rejoice and burst into
    flower.
Let it flower with fields of
    asphodel,
let it rejoice and shout for joy.
The glory of Lebanon is given to it,
the splendour too of Carmel and
    Sharon;
these will see the glory of the LORD,
the splendour of our God.

Brace the arms that are limp,
steady the knees that give way;
say to the anxious, 'Be strong, fear
    not!
Your God comes to save you
with his vengeance and his
    retribution.'
Then the eyes of the blind will be
    opened,
and the ears of the deaf unstopped.
Then the lame will leap like deer,
and the dumb shout aloud;
for water will spring up in the
    wilderness

and torrents flow in the desert.
The mirage will become a pool,
the thirsty land bubbling springs;
instead of reeds and rushes, grass
    will grow
in country where wolves have their
    lairs.

And a causeway will appear there;
It will be called the Way of Holiness.
No one unclean will pass along it;
it will become a pilgrim's way,
and no fool will trespass on it.
No lion will come there,
no savage beast go by;
not one will be found there.
But by that way those the LORD has
    redeemed will return.
The LORD's people, set free, will come
    back
and enter Zion with shouts of
    triumph,
crowned with everlasting joy.
Gladness and joy will come upon
    them,
while suffering and weariness flee
    away.

Comments on the Story

Isaiah 35 brings to closure the edited work of the Isaiah who was called to testify in the eighth century B.C.E. Attached to the work of the eighth-century prophet is the four chapter unit, 36–39, which serves as a historical appendix. The four chapters in the appendix are virtually a duplicate of 2 Kings 18:13–20:19.

The words of Isaiah 35 bring a welcome contrast to those of the preceding chapter. There, in a proclamation of destruction, we witness the downfall of God's enemies, a virtual collapse of the cosmic order, and the destruction in particular of Edom, one of those border states on the edge of Judah. The metaphors found in the chapter are images of sacrifice and slaughter that leave the land blood-soaked. The continual string of words that describes Yahweh's emotion, Yahweh's rage and fury, in concert with the description of how that rage and fury will be made manifest in the land, leaves the reader with an eerie discomfort. The description of the devastation of Edom (34:8-17) describes the monarchy whose new name shall be "No Kingdom There." It will become nothing.

Isaiah 35 abruptly brings a different and joyous word about the restoration of Zion. With imagery somewhat akin to that of Second and Third Isaiah (though the debate about the relationship between this chapter and the later Isaiahs is not conclusive), the chapter describes a ring of "homecoming" in the air; the people are returning to Zion. The images of Isaiah 35 are reminiscent of the Israelites' journey from Egypt to the land of promise, yet this journey will be more wonder-filled. The new exodus will exceed the old.

The chapter begins with a description of the land that will be transformed. The wilderness, dry land, and the desert will become fertile (v. 1). They will be given glory and majesty. "They shall see the glory of the LORD, the majesty of our God" (v. 2 NRSV). The readers wonder—"Who are they?" Who will see Yahweh's glory—Is it the wilderness, the dry land and the desert? Is it those who will make their way through the once barren land? It is this question— "Who will see the glory?" that will provide for the storyteller an entree into a text that is relevant and appropriate for any community hopeful and wanting significant change.

The unit proceeds by sending a message to those who are in need of salvation. The word from the prophet is that they should not fear; they should be strong (v. 4). The storyteller will not find it difficult to find images of those with "weak hands" and "feeble knees." Nor will it be difficult to conjure portraits of those with "fearful hearts." It is to these that this song is sung (vv. 3-4). It will be a bigger challenge to convince the hearers that they can be strong because God will come and save them.

But then, the entire text in verses 1-10 of Isaiah 35 is filled with the unbelievable. Blind eyes are opened, unhearing ears are unstopped, the lame leap, the mute sing, the wilderness breaks forth in water and the desert in streams. There will be a clear pathway for God's people, none shall go astray, and there will be no dangerous animals. And the people will return to their wonderful Zion, singing, joyful, and glad. All of their sorrow and sighing shall flee away (vv. 9-10).

Isaiah 35 is found twice in the three-year lectionary—once in Advent and once in the long season of Pentecost. No doubt, different hopes and different needs will come to mind as the text is read through the lens of these dissimilar liturgical seasons. Whenever it is read, one wonders if there is anything that can mar this grand and glorious vision of what will, someday, come to be.

For the contemporary storyteller, perhaps there is one blemish, because the question of *who* will see the glory of Yahweh continues to haunt us. We look through the text for clues to the answer. Who will be in this great procession to Zion? God's people will be there (v. 8), the redeemed shall walk there (v. 9), and the ransomed of Yahweh (v. 10) are those who will be returning to Zion with joy. We thrill because it seems that the path has been made ready and been made safe for all travelers. We are disappointed. Sadly, the unclean will not be allowed to travel there. In this grand and glorious vision of what is to come—couldn't *all* be welcomed to make the journey?

We know that we probably criticize too quickly. We know that our "inclusive" vision also is marred by myopic and unfocused perspective. Yet we are challenged by this text to think of this grand and glorious procession of God's people and to ask ourselves—Who in *our* vision is not present? We see the highway stretched out before us through a land filled with running streams of cool water, but who is forbidden to be there?

Retelling the Story

Late in the afternoon, as the Farmer worked the dry land, he had a vision. It wasn't an illusion of heat shimmering out of the dry land or the spectre created by an overworked mind. It was a projection, a vision of what the land would be like. The great irrigation ditches were repaired, and stones to ease the erosion added with much labor. Now the great river, never quite tamed, was usable. Someday its vast cool wetness would embrace the Farmer's fields again. He could see in his mind the crops feeding the hungry. Those sickened by the processes of the drought would now be made well as the nutrients in the grain and vegetables fed the body. He had always been proud of his work and often heard people say with some small pride, "I never complain about the Farmer with my mouth full!"

As he thought about the great mass of people becoming healthy from his hard work, the image shifted unbidden in his mind. The field became the multitude. He saw, clearly now, their real hunger. The hunger was of their soul. He saw diseases and infirmities caused, not by plague and drought, but by a true emptiness. Not the emptiness of their stomachs, but of their souls. The weakness was not of body, but spirit.

He despaired as he saw the vision. How could he water their souls and feed their hearts? He was no prophet, no speaker of healing words. He was the Farmer.

Then, in his mind, he saw himself feeding and healing the multitude. Even as he fed them bread and gave them cool water, the bread and water changed and became words. Words that healed, words that fed, words that satisfied. Water that never ended, bread that fed a multitude without end. He fed them not with visions of his own or his cleverness of speech. He fed them, healed them, by simply repeating the words the Prophet spoke.

Could such a thing be? And then he remembered the words of the vision.

Who do I send? Who goes for me?

And the Farmer said: *Here am I! Send me. (R. Michael Sanders)*

The sages say that when Solomon was building the Temple there was a place set aside for fruit trees that produced all sorts of gold-colored fruit. When the fruit fell to the ground, the priests had enough and more than they needed. When the Temple fell and the invaders entered the place where the trees were planted, the fruit withered and the trees did not bear. When Isaiah said, "Let the wilderness and the parched land be glad, let the desert places rejoice and burst into flower," it was God's promise that the fruit trees on the Temple grounds would once more produce fruit. It was the promise that the people would return and worship again in the Holy City. (*Sefer Ha-Aggadah* 125. 116)

The Word and Words

Jeremiah, son of a priest, is born to become a prophet, and he reluctantly accepts the commission.

The Story

THE words of Jeremiah son of Hilkiah, one of the priests at Anathoth in Benjamin. The word of the LORD came to him in the thirteenth year of the reign of Josiah son of Amon, king of Judah. It came also during the reign of Jehoiakim son of Josiah, king of Judah, until the end of the eleventh year of Zedekiah son of Josiah, king of Judah. In the fifth month the inhabitants of Jerusalem were carried off into exile.

THIS word of the LORD came to me: 'Before I formed you in the womb I chose you, and before you were born I consecrated you; I appointed you a prophet to the nations.' 'Ah! Lord GOD,' I answered, 'I am not skilled in speaking; I am too young.' But the LORD said, 'Do not plead that you are too young; for you are to go to whatever people I send you, and say whatever I tell you to say. Fear none of them, for I shall be with you to keep you safe.' This was the word of the LORD. Then the LORD stretched out his hand, and touching my mouth said to me, 'See, I put my words into your mouth. This day I give you authority over nations and kingdoms to uproot and to pull down, to destroy and to demolish, to build and to plant.'

Comments on the Story

As Jeremiah's story begins, he is introduced to and defined for the reader by his relationships. We are told that he is the son of Hilkiah, a priest. He has a relationship to the priests of Anathoth, a city in the land of Benjamin just north of Jerusalem. The story is given a historical context; we are told where the story takes place, and we are given the names of the rulers of Judah—Josiah, Jehoiakim, and Zedekiah—who rule during Jeremiah's prophetic career. Those familiar with the history of Judah would know that Jeremiah's career, then, perhaps began in a time of hopefulness and optimism when the good king Josiah was leading the people back to their fundamental covenant with Yahweh. His prophetic career ended when Jerusalem was taken captive—from prosperity to devastation, from community to exile. The story of Jeremiah is a painful one; he is deeply affected by what he sees, and throughout his years as prophet he knows that the end of the good days is possible, at times he thinks inevitable. Jeremiah is thrust into the story of a national demise.

The stage is set and abruptly Jeremiah receives a word, a call from Yahweh. We know nothing about his life before the word was given to him; it is as if what happened before is not important. Simply the word intrudes and in first person Jeremiah recounts it for the reader/hearer. The story is the detailing of the conversation between Jeremiah and the One who has called him. The description is terse; irrelevancies are suppressed. The author provides for us only what we need to know—who is called, who is calling. Had there been conversations between Jeremiah and this Yahweh before? We do not know. It is as if at this moment life begins for Jeremiah, as if he has come into the world for no other purpose.

Who is the one who has called? The one who calls Jeremiah is the one who has created Jeremiah, and who now consecrates and appoints him. "Before I formed you" the speech begins. Before he was even conceived, Jeremiah was known and a part of God's plan. Was he frightened to discover that he was known so intimately, so completely? He is consecrated and appointed to be a prophet. The call, however, is not yet a specific one. Jeremiah is not told where he will go, what he will speak, or whom he will address. The one who is known is sent to the unknown.

The hesitant reply of Jeremiah is both familiar (as witnessed in the response of other prophets who receive a call from Yahweh) and understandable. He does not feel capable; on the basis of both his inexperience and his youth he does not feel qualified for the task. The confession of weakness provides the opportunity for divine words of encouragement. In a couplet, Jeremiah is told to "go" where he is sent and to "speak" what is commanded—with the assistance of Yahweh's continual presence. The storyteller is reminded that often in the Old Testament the divine response to human anxiety is, as here, "Do not be afraid, . . . for I am with you" (see Deut. 20:1, 31:8; Isa. 41:10 NRSV). The same God who calls also reaches out, protects, and delivers. The divine word of hope is the antidote to despair.

Yahweh reaches out and touches Jeremiah's mouth (v. 9). As with the prophet Isaiah whose lips were purified, Jeremiah is made ready to speak. There is an intimacy between God and prophet, the message and the messenger. Words are put into the prophet's mouth; they are a gift from God. Unlike Isaiah (chapter 6), Ezekiel (chapter 1), and Amos (chapter 7), Jeremiah has received no vision; he has been called by the word, and he has been given "word" to carry out his mission.

The reader is reminded as she reads the first chapter of Jeremiah that the word is something with power. With only the words that are put into his mouth by Yahweh, Jeremiah will be appointed over nations and kingdoms, he will pluck up and pull down the nations. Four verbs describe his mission; he will destroy, overthrow, build, and plant (v. 10 NRSV). All this he will do with words—dynamic, vital, life-changing words.

As listeners of the narrative we are overwhelmed by the power bestowed on this young one who does not feel adequate to speak for Yahweh. Because he is given the word and the promise of God's presence as he delivers that word, we would never anticipate that the task he has been given would bring such despair. The word of Jeremiah will not go unopposed. We are alerted in verse 18 to the overwhelming obstacles that will be facing the spokesperson—he will have to face the whole land, the kings of Judah, the princes, priests and all the people who will be fighting against him. We know that he has been called, and we want him to persevere, to bring the truth of Yahweh. We are saddened to find as we read his indictments against the community, that we, along with the community in Jerusalem, are guilty of the social evils that he names. We know about oppression, violence, destruction, the abuse of power, and the neglect of others in the community. We know about idolatry and injustice and the motives from which they both arrive. The words sting, and centuries after they were first spoken we feel their power. Hopefully his words will pluck up, pull down, destroy, and overthrow what is ungodly among us. Hopefully his words can be used to build and plant the faithful world that God intended for us.

The story of Jeremiah's call to prophesy incorporates two visions (vv. 11-12 and 13-14) one of an almond tree and one of the boiling pot. Both begin as the call to prophesy began in verse 4—"The word of the LORD came" (NRSV). God does not encourage the prophet to speak God's word by trivializing the work. God makes no promise that the work will be easy or even safe. Immediately God speaks to Jeremiah through these visions, making it clear that the message that will be sent to God's people will be neither pleasant nor welcome. Yet, the promise remains and it is reiterated for the prophet who must be overwhelmed by the tasks before him. God will be present. "I am with you, says the LORD, to deliver you" (v. 19 NRSV).

Retelling the Story

Excerpt from the journal of Baruch, a scribe:

There are times in one's life after which nothing will ever be the same. Such a time for me was the day I was first called into the service of the priest Jeremiah bar Hilkiah. Though that first meeting took place many years ago I remember it as if it had happened this morning. I was often called upon to serve among the priestly orders. Most of them were too busy with holy things to bother with learning to write. Mostly I was engaged to make lists of supplies or schedules of service, pretty boring stuff, all in all. When the messenger came that morning long ago I gathered up the tools of my trade and followed, expecting just another ordinary assignment.

Nothing could have been farther from what I encountered when I arrived. My new employer sat staring off into space as if he had been stunned by a blow to the forehead. I spoke to him asking what his pleasure would be that morning. He remained silent for a long time, so long that I thought perhaps he was in a trance. When he finally did speak he muttered under his breath, "No pleasure."

"Excuse me?" I replied but he spoke again as if I had said nothing.

"Write this," he began, "The words of Jeremiah, son of Hilkiah, a priest of Anathoth in Benjamin. The word of the YHWH . . . " As soon as these words came out of his mouth I knew this was going to be no usual task. My intuition was correct since from that day to this there has been nothing ordinary about my service to this extraordinary man.

"This is the word of YHWH that came to me. While your mother was weaving your first baby blanket I was weaving you together in her womb, choosing you to reveal a special pattern in your life. While she was praying for a healthy birth I was setting you apart for a sacred task. You will speak my words to many nations. 'Do not do this to me, I pray. I am no speaker and besides, I am too young for such a calling.' I replied.

When the prophets found reasons that they should not be called to be God's messengers, God always had an answer ready for them. The sages tell that God replied, "Do you think I have no other avenues to get my word out but you? If I so choose, my word can be spoken by a snake, or a scorpion, or a frog." (*Sefer Ha-Aggadah* 480.101)

God told Jeremiah that he had been chosen when still in his mother's womb to be a prophet. Jeremiah was not so sure about his calling at first. He complained that there had never been a prophet in Israel who had not suffered humiliation at the hands of those to whom he was to prophesy. The people who were led out of Egypt by Moses complained about his leadership. Later, others made fun of Elijah's frizzy hair and conversely ridiculed Elisha because he was bald.

Then Jeremiah told God that he could not be a prophet because he was as yet just a child. God answered, "That is the very reason I love you so, because you are a child." (*Sefer Ha-Aggadah* 478.84)

"The voice of YHWH came again saying, 'You are as old as you need to be, and as for the words you will say, leave them to me. Just speak the words I tell you to say. My words will live on your tongue for I will birth them there.' Then the hand of YHWH reached out and touched my mouth. 'See, I have put the words in your mouth. These words have my authority behind them. They will uproot kingdoms and pull down nations. At the same time though they will have the power to plant the new where the old has been pulled up and to build where the old has been demolished.' "

He stared off into space like a madman. "I have seen the almond tree of God's determination to punish and the cauldron of God's fire flaming high, stirred bright by the North wind."

Of course, I understood none of this. Whether this man was possessed by a spirit or wrestling with God only one wiser and more discerning than I could tell. I was terrified and fascinated at the same time. I would not have been shocked if the man had burst into flames himself right there before my eyes. When I came to my senses again he was saying over and over in a loud voice, "Brace yourself, Jeremiah. Brace yourself."

I thought, "Brace yourself, Baruch; this is going to be a rough ride."

The ancient rabbis discerned a similar pattern among all the prophets. Though they began their prophetic utterances with evidence proving why Israel deserved to be punished, they always concluded with God's own words of comfort. (*Sefer Ha-Aggadah* 478.90)

If it will be a holy one as well, only time would tell. To tell you the truth, my first impulse was to gather up my writing instruments and run as far away from this madman as I could go. But by some deeper intuition, divine or human I cannot say, I stayed seated, and continued writing the words he spoke and have remained in his service to this day. (Michael E. Williams)

Remember When . . .

Jeremiah accuses his people of deserting their heritage—their ancestral stories—by defiling their promised homeland.

The Story

Listen to the word of the LORD, people of Jacob, all you families of Israel. These are the words of the LORD:

What fault did your forefathers find
in me,
that they went so far astray from me,
pursuing worthless idols
and becoming worthless like them;
that they did not ask, 'Where is the
LORD,
who brought us up from Egypt
and led us through the wilderness,
through a barren and broken
country,
a country parched and forbidding,
where no one ever travelled,
where no one made his home?'
I brought you into a fertile land
to enjoy its fruit and every good
thing in it;
but when you entered my land you
defiled it
and made loathsome the home I gave
you.
The priests no longer asked, 'Where
is the LORD?'
Those who handled the law had no
real knowledge of me,
the shepherds of the people rebelled
against me;

the prophets prophesied in the name
of Baal
and followed gods who were
powerless to help.

Therefore I shall bring a charge
against you once more,
says the LORD,
against you and against your
descendants.
Cross to the coasts and islands of
Kittim and see,
send to Kedar and observe closely,
see whether there has been anything
like this:
has a nation ever exchanged its gods,
and these no gods at all?
Yet my people have exchanged their
glory
for a god altogether powerless.
Be aghast at this, you heavens,
shudder in utter horror,
says the LORD.
My people have committed two sins:
they have rejected me,
a source of living water,
and they have hewn out for
themselves cisterns,
cracked cisterns which hold no
water.

Comments on the Story

Jeremiah 2:4-13 is located in a larger unit that follows the story of Jeremiah's call and introduces the edited book by summarizing the prophet's message to the unfaithful Judah. More particularly, Jeremiah 2:1–4:4 is a series of accusations against the nation. Though Jeremiah 2:4-13 is not itself a narrative, the prophet reminds those he addresses of a story—the story of their ancestors. The prophet knows that when the people forget their story, life becomes at least distorted and perhaps perverted. Allusions to the land of Egypt, the wilderness wanderings and the entry into Canaan are brief. But only very cursory reminders are needed to bring the epic of Moses and the deliverance of the Israelites from slavery to consciousness. What is the point of the telling of the story? As usual in the prophetic material, the story serves as a reminder to the community that Yahweh has been faithful in the past—this in contrast to their own lack of faithfulness in the present. Not that the people have always been faithless! In its present context this oracle for the house of Jacob and all the families of the house of Israel is preceded by words of remembering; Yahweh is remembering a time when the people were faithful and devoted, when they loved him as a bride loves. Yahweh remembers a time when they were holy (vv. 2-3).

Abruptly, then, our series of oracles begins; it is a series of oracles brought together for a theological purpose. The series begins with the rhetorical questioning of Yahweh who asks, "What wrong did your ancestors find in me?" That could be, for Yahweh, the only explanation for their faithlessness—there was a wrong committed against them. But the history is recounted, the story is told and there is *no* wrong. Yahweh has been faithful in guiding and protecting the community on its journey from the old land to the new. Yahweh brought them up from the land of Egypt, led them in the wilderness filled with desert land and pits, a land of deep darkness, a land so barren that no one could live there. And Yahweh brought them to a land of bounty filled with fruits and good things. Contrast is used to highlight the distinctions between the land through which the Israelites traveled and the land to which they were led.

Yahweh led them through the arid land of deep darkness to the fruitful land filled with good things. As this story is recounted, the same indictment appears twice—first against the general community (v. 6) and later (v. 8) against the priests. They had not asked "Where is the Lord?" The sin of the community is that, as they have gone about life, they have not looked for Yahweh in their midst.

The leadership is not exempt. Rather, they are singled out for accusation. The priests who were responsible for the purity of worship did not know Yahweh, the rulers transgressed, and the prophets prophesied by Baal (v. 8). They went after things that did not "profit gods that were powerless." Of interest to the storyteller is this recurring reference to things that do not profit, the "worthless" nature of the people and their pursuits (vv. 4, 8, 11). Translations have dealt with this intriguing notion of worthlessness in a variety of ways. Worthless things have been translated as phantoms and delusions. Pursuing them the people have become empty or deluded. They amused themselves to death. In essence, the people have no real substance. The ancestors went far from Yahweh and went after "worthless" things, things that were insubstantial or vain. Thus they became "worthless" themselves. No doubt the prophet speaks of the following after other gods (v. 11a). The people have exchanged their glory for something that does not profit—again something that is worthless and powerless.

Lest the point not be grasped, the unit ends with a vital metaphor that graphically illustrates the ultimate in worthlessness. The people have dug cisterns; the cisterns are cracked and thus can hold no water. The people have abandoned the "fountain of living water" for no water. They have deprived themselves of the life-giving liquid. What good are cracked cisterns? What good are the people of Yahweh when they are not faithful people of Yahweh? Both are worthless.

Yahweh brings the accusation against the people (v. 9). Yahweh cannot understand the choices that the people have made. The heavens are called to be utterly shocked. Nothing like this has ever occurred in the east or in the west (v. 10). Never has a nation before changed its gods; never before has a nation exchanged glory for something that did not profit. Those who were once led through the land of dry desert and wilderness by the fountain of living water now find themselves in the land of plenty but they have nothing to drink. How did these people come to turn away from their exclusive loyalty to their God—the one and only God who has been formative in their history?

The storyteller is called to bring to the listeners the folly of putting faith in worthless things while walking through life blinded to the one who is worthy of our attention. Perhaps the people were not aware that their time and energy and devotion were going toward worthless things. We can often deceive ourselves about the value of our priorities. The storyteller can invite the hearer to examine his or her life and ask—As I walk through life, where is the Lord?

Verses 14-19 describe the results of the people's faithlessness. They are in despair. The nation has become enslaved to other nations. Their life is evil and bitter (v. 19).

We as hearers of the "story" watch the community of God's people walk resolutely toward their own demise. We remember how the story began in verses 2-3 as the teller recounted for the reader words about Israel's early devotion. Verses 4-13 then describe the people's turning away from Yahweh to go after worthless things. Verses 14-19 describe the tragic consequences of such a life. We are invited to locate ourselves in this story.

81

Retelling the Story

"Welcome to today's seminar. You've paid a hefty fee to be here. If you have felt like a loser too long or just want to get more out of your life, you've come to the right place. If you've lived on too little for too long and want to be rich beyond your wildest dreams, you've come to the right place. If you're sick and tired of serving the needs of other people and want to take charge of your own life and destiny, then you've come to the right place.

"Bud Avarice has the answers for all the questions in your life. You've all read his best-selling book, *The Seven Secrets of the Fabulously Successful,* and you want to know more. Well, when you leave here today you will be heading toward easy street. But you didn't come here to listen to me. You came to hear the secrets of success from the success guru himself, Dr. Bud Avarice. So without further delay, it is my pleasure to present to you the best-selling author of *Forget the Past and Believe in Yourself: Your Path to Personal Power,* Dr. Bud Avarice."

(*Wild applause!*)

> The sages saw God's healing and liberating hand at work in many ways in the story of the Exodus. Some of the workers must have been maimed as they made the bricks for the Egyptians. Surely some of the bricks or even stones had fallen and permanently harmed some workers. Since God did not wish to give the Torah to a people so broken by their enslavement, the angels were called upon to heal them. And so they did. At least that is what some rabbis say. (S*efer Ha-Aggadah* 78.26)

"Are you a loser or a winner? The answer is up to you. You hold your destiny in your own hands, and today I am here to teach you how to reach out and take hold of your future. There is a fabulously successful person inside you waiting to get out. I don't care what you have believed in for your entire life. From now on you are the center of your own universe. It doesn't matter how God created you, today is the day you re-create yourself in the image of success. Don't get stuck with the old photographs from the past. Don't get stuck replaying the old tapes from the past. The first secret of the fabulously successful is to forget the past. The only thing you have to remember is that today is the first day of the rest of your life.

"The second secret of the fabulously successful is that they make themselves number one. Nothing and no one else can take the seat at the center of your life but you. Put yourself and your needs in the center ring and you are on your way.

"The third secret of those people the world envies is that after they put their desires at the center of their universe they look out for themselves first, last, and always. When they come to an important decision in their lives they always ask, "What do I get out of it?" And if the deal doesn't have the payoff, they give it the brush-off. Not a soul in the universe can be as important as you are, if you intend to be fabulously successful.

"The fourth secret of those who succeed is that success must be more important than anything else in your life. There are plenty of slobs who put their spouses and children before their success and look where they wind up. They are at the bottom of the heap. If you think your wife's career or your husband's surgery or your kid's kindergarten program is as important as your meeting with a client, then you can leave the room right now. Because if anything is more important than your success, you were not cut out to be fabulously successful.

"The fifth secret of the fabulously successful is that they make everything pay. If you can't write off a church or charity on your income tax, don't give them anything. If your brother-in-law needs a helping hand, make sure you get at least two points above the going interest rate. And make sure you have some ex–football player friends to put on the pressure at collection time.

> If the children of Israel had no weavers to come out of slavery with them, how did they clothe themselves during the wilderness wanderings? Some of the sages suggest that God had the angels make clothes for them. These marvelous clothes never wore out and never needed cleaning. The pillar of fire that led the people by night cleaned their garments as they walked. Such was the extent of God's love for these freed slaves. (*Sefer Ha-Aggadah* 99.121)

"The sixth secret of the fabulously successful is to know that people who are poor deserve to be poor. Losers choose to be losers. But you took the first step toward being a winner when you enrolled in this seminar. Winners think like winners and act like winners. Winners don't associate with losers and they certainly don't offer them a helping hand. All this 'everybody get together and love one another' is fine—for losers. But you don't want to let a loser drag you down to his level. Winners don't need help, and winners don't give help.

"Finally, the seventh secret of the fabulously successful is to give people whatever they want—for a price. You can't worry if something you sell is going to hurt or kill someone. After all, you didn't make them buy it. It's not your responsibility. It's theirs. The problem with the world today is that people don't want to take responsibility for their own actions. So you can say with a clear conscience that those who harm themselves from your product made their own bed, now they can sleep in it, maybe forever. . . ." *(Michael E. Williams)*

Uncreated

The prophet imagines urban blight for the chosen City of God, which is melting before the whirlwind of torment.

The Story

At that time this people and
Jerusalem will be told:

A scorching wind from the desert
   heights
sweeps down on my people;
it is no breeze for winnowing or for
   cleansing.
A wind too strong for these
will come at my bidding,
and now I shall state my case against
   my people.

. . . .

I looked at the earth, and it was
   chaos,
at the heavens, and their light was
   gone,
at the mountains, and they were
   reeling,

and all the hills rocked to and fro.
I looked: no one was there,
and all the birds of heaven had taken
   wing.
I looked: the fertile land was
   wilderness,
its towns all razed to the ground
before the LORD, before his fierce
   anger.
These are the words of the LORD:
The whole land will be desolate,
and I shall make an end of it.
The earth will be in mourning for
   this
and the heavens above turn black;
for I have made known my purpose,
and I shall not relent or change it.

Comments on the Story

Jeremiah 4 begins with a call to Israel to "return" to Yahweh. The plea to return is repeated in verse 1 to demonstrate the urgency and intensity of the appeal. If the people do not return, there are consequences. The foe from the north, a common thematic element in Jeremiah, will come to destroy them. The chapter continues with words and visions from the prophet about the coming devastation.

Two segments of chapter 4 are found in the list of lectionary texts. The first is the brief oracle found in Jeremiah 4:11-12, an oracle whose form reminds the reader of a special news bulletin or the headlines on the front page of the morning newspaper: "A hot wind comes out of the bare heights toward the poor people." Thus begins the oracle that spells out disaster for the city of Jerusalem and its residents. Though embedded in a series of oracles with similar motifs of judgment and destruction, the oracle in verses 11-12 uses unusual imagery to depict the coming of the angry Yahweh. The hot wind (or spirit!) comes from Yahweh out of the desert; it is a wind that is too strong to winnow or to cleanse, a wind much too strong for either.

This terse announcement of imminent destruction is followed by a description of the whirlwind as it comes closer and closer to the community. The reader can sense the fright and the desperation of the one who is watching, the one who pronounces the woe upon the community and who calls Jerusalem to cleanse itself so that it might be saved. The prophet is calling for the city to cleanse itself *now*! The consequent wailing and lamenting of the prophet and the city's inhabitants (vv. 19-22) who are experiencing devastation precede the second assigned lectionary text—4:23-28. These verses recount the vision of the prophet: destruction has come. Only the prophet remains to see the ruined Jerusalem.

The vision begins with the prophet imagining what the devastated land would look like. "I looked. . . . " The three following verses begin in identical fashion, each recounting for the reader part of the horror that the prophet experiences: waste and void, the quaking of mountains, the total absence of humanity, ruined cities and desert. By using the phrase "waste and void" the author reminds the listener/reader of the condition of the universe before God created the earth (Gen. 1:1). It is as if the world has returned to the primordial chaos and confusion that was before the world's creation (Gen. 1:1). By reiterating these words from the creation story, the prophet underscores what he observes—all that was created by God and seen to be good is now destroyed. By their actions and their unfaithfulness, the people of God have "uncreated" the world.

What would it be like to be the "sole survivor" in a destroyed and devastated city? The vision of the prophet takes on this fictive quality. The prophet sees the waste and the void. There is darkness. The foundation of the city is not firm, there is quaking. No humanity. Even the birds have left. There is the aura of death. It is quiet. The vegetation has withered—what was once fruitful has become like desert. The city is in ruins.

It is not difficult for the contemporary storyteller to relate to this vision of the desolate city. While the contemporary city is not void of humanity, there can be in the city the overwhelming sense of death and decay, of rust and smog. Though there is, in the strict sense of the word "life"—there are many who seem to have no life—no real life, no abundant life. Those who dare to live or sojourn there do give accounts of unanticipated experiences of beauty and glimpses of grace. There are, however, few such moments in these words from Jeremiah. Actually, there is only one. Yahweh reports that while the whole land seems desolate, the land will not come to "full end." This one oblique and difficult reference to a potential future for the city is quickly swallowed by the more pessimistic picture of the earth mourning, black heavens and the words of Yahweh who adamantly states once again that there will be no relenting or turning back. There is little now that can be done (vv. 27-28). The storyteller wonders if the story has come to a disastrous and inevitable end.

Chapter 4 comes to closure with the city itself, personified as a woman in labor, crying out in anguish. Her hands are outstretched, life is coming to an end. This picture of the devastation of the city is followed by a command. Someone, everyone, is to run urgently through the city. In a series of imperatives—run, look, take note, search, and see—they are commanded to look for just *one* person who acts justly and seeks truth. If just one person is found, the city can be pardoned. One person can turn the tide.

We wonder about this promise. Would Yahweh save the city because one just person is found there? Why? And while we struggle with the theological implications of the word Yahweh speaks, we do know in our hearts that one voice, one voice speaking and demanding justice, could make a difference. We, like Jeremiah, feel too inadequate to be the one.

Retelling the Story

Excerpt from the journal of Baruch, a scribe:

It was as if I had awakened from a dream only to find I was in the midst of yet another dream. I had been recording all night when the prophet finally allowed himself some rest. Consequently, I was able to sleep on the floor next to the fire. In the middle of the night I heard weeping and wailing and such sounds as I never before heard from human lips. Of course I knew immediately whose terrified voice it was and suspected it would only be a matter of time before I heard an account of the horrific vision that had torn him from his sleep.

I learned more than I ever wanted to know of these terrors much sooner than I thought. I had just turned my face toward the dying warmth of the fire when Jeremiah came tearing into the room, his hair disheveled and his face so clearly aghast that I thought for an instant he was wearing a mask. He sat and said nothing for a long time. The grimace of his face set in high relief by shadows from the fire told of horrors unspeakable. I stoked the fire and the brighter flames only served to intensify his despairing visage.

"Take this down," he spoke, "I will blow my hot breath and scorch the earth. No winnowing or cleaning breeze for grain is this, but by this wind I will winnow my people and cleanse them. This hot desert wind

will make Jerusalem a place of desolation and in its ruins I will prosecute my people."

Jeremiah paused and I, in turn, ceased my writing with his last word. "Baruch," he was looking at me as he addressed me now, "imagine you alone survive the destruction of a whirlwind. You awaken one morning and during the night all has been swept away as surely as if a divine hand had reached out and decimated it. You cast your eyes upward and the light of the sun is

From the very start, the rabbis say, people were so dishonest that it was almost impossible to tell what our true nature was. They say that humanity was like a young fig tree that sprouted thorns before fruit ever appeared. At times like that you do begin to wonder if its nature is to produce thorns only, or if the fruit will ever appear. This is how we must sometimes appear to God. (*Sefer Ha-Aggadah* 8.15)

cloaked in sandstorm brown. You look to the mountains and they are trembling at their very foundations. You look to the seas and they are churning in their very depths like a pot of water boiling. There is no human habitation visible anywhere on the earth. There is no place of worship visible anywhere on the earth. There is no bird or tree visible over the whole face of the earth. There is no fish or creature of the land visible over the whole face of the earth.

"The heat of the wind has scorched every living thing and killed it to its root. The breath of God has taken the breath from every creature that breathed. Even the earth that for generations has brought forth abundance for the people lies baked and cracked. The ground that brought forth life lies a corpse at your feet. Imagine that, Baruch, if you can."

I did my best to follow the prophet's instruction, but, I admit, my imagination could not stretch to encompass such desolation. Yet every crease of Jeremiah's face stood ready to verify every word he had spoken. "I alone am left to tell this sad, sad tale," his face seemed to cry out. "I alone am left to tune this dirge for that which is forever lost."

I asked if I was to record what

One rabbi suggested that people should try to live in a city that was not very old. Since it had not been around very long, it had not had as much time to offend God with its sins. Perhaps such a city would escape the fate that Jeremiah described. (*Sefer Ha-Aggadah* 749.265)

he had described to me. Or is this a grief too deep for words? When he spoke again I could not tell if he had heard me and was answering, or if

The sages say that God takes no pleasure in punishing anyone. That is why in each generation an advocate was chosen to argue the case on behalf of the people. That is why Jeremiah was told to search the highways and byways to see if there was one just individual to serve as an advocate for the people. The people were not left to find their own attorney. Rather, one was appointed by God for them. (*Sefer Ha-Aggadah* 557.207)

he was simply continuing his tragic commentary where he had left off. "The sky will wear mourning's dark dress and the very stones will cry out their grief. The sadness of God will rock the universe from top to bottom like a mourner weeping. And I alone will be left to speak about God's broken heart to the empty air, to the broken earth."

Then the prophet wept. So long and hard did he weep that I feared he would die from his sorrow. I caught what words I could and wrote them down. I captured the gist of what he said, but no words in a human tongue have been invented to describe such heart-rending sadness. As a mother weeps at the loss of her child, so did Jeremiah weep for Jerusalem, so did God weep for these beloved children.

While words can never say exactly what happened that day, I will always carry with me the residue of this grief beneath which I still hear the whispers of unrequited love. (Michael E. Williams)

Death to the One I Love

With the bones of dead people piled in heaps across the devastated land, all who remain—the people, God, and the prophet—wail and scream in sorrowful suffering.

The Story

There is no cure for my grief;
I am sick at heart.
Hear my people's cry of distress
from a distant land:
'Is the LORD not in Zion?
Is her King no longer there?'
Why do they provoke me with their
images
and with their futile foreign gods?
Harvest is past, summer is over,
and we are not saved.
I am wounded by my people's
wound;

I go about in mourning, overcome
with horror.
Is there no balm in Gilead,
no physician there?
Why has no new skin grown over
their wound?
Would that my head were a spring
of water,
my eyes a fountain of tears,
that I might weep day and night
for the slain of my people.

Comments on the Story

Jeremiah 8 is filled with provocative and disturbing imagery that describes the plight of the people of God who have been unfaithful to God. The primary visual image for verses 1-3 is that of the bones of the kings, officials, priests, prophets, and inhabitants of Jerusalem. The bones are spread on the barren ground, neither gathered nor buried. The imagery is of death. Following these verses there comes a messenger formula "Thus says the Lord. . . " and a series of indictments against the community:

Verses 4-7—Indictment. These verses are descriptive of a people who do not do what is natural; what is natural is for the people to *turn back* to Yahweh. But what is described is a people who go astray and do not *turn back* (v. 4). They are people intent on deceit and who refuse to *return* (v. 5). There is none who will *turn back* from wickedness (v. 6). Even the birds—the stork, turtledove, swallow, and the crane know instinctively the seasons in which they migrate from one place to another and return to the place from which they have come. In like manner, those who "migrated" away from Yahweh, those who have experienced Yahweh's blessing, should naturally return.

Verses 8-9—Indictment. These verses question the wisdom of a people who think they are wise. Those claiming wisdom have in reality rejected the word of Yahweh. They have cried out that there is peace in the land, when there is none.

Verses 10-13—Threat. The consequences of the people's behavior are laid out before them. "Therefore" (vv. 10 and 12) announces what now will befall this community. The threats are interwoven with further indictments—prophets and priests have cried peace when there was none, and were not ashamed. They did not blush. The people are compared to the unfruitful vine. There are no grapes, no figs, even the leaves of the vine have withered. The unfaithful people of Yahweh are not productive covenantal partners.

Verses 14-17—Tragedy unfolds. Perhaps the most chilling imagery comes in verses 14-17 where finally the people speak. They perceive Yahweh as a God who has doomed them to perish. It is as if they have been given poisoned water to drink, as if Yahweh has let poisoned snakes out loose among them. The rhetoric effectively betrays the panic and the urgency of those who can no longer avoid the prophetic word. There is no healing; there is terror as the predicted devastation comes to pass.

This vast panorama of imagery is prelude to the lectionary text (8:18–9:1) in which we observe the movement to lament. The anger of Yahweh and the despair of the community bring uncontrollable grief to the prophet who loves *both* Yahweh and people. He hears the cry of the people from across the land; he also hears the cry of Yahweh who cannot understand why the people have continued to provoke his anger. The prophet stands between the people and Yahweh and with the people. The cries from both are deafening. He finds that his joy is gone and his heart is sick. The hurt of the people has become his own (v. 21).

It is difficult in chapter 8 to determine clear beginnings and endings to units. It is difficult to determine who is speaking and to whom. But this confusion underscores the profound and immense emotional experience of each character in the drama. Grief blurs vision. Boundaries become unclear and speech comes spontaneously. In times of lament and mourning there are often uncontrollable outpourings of grief. When one speech ends, or even before one ends, another begins, so that sounds blend and there is a never ending roar of weeping and wailing. The laments of the prophet and of God become indistinguishable. It is the immense sadness we feel when we cannot help or heal another. "Is there no balm in Gilead? Is there no physician there" (8:22 NRSV)? Is there nowhere these people can turn? The prophet feels helpless and hopeless. God feels helpless and hopeless.

> O that my head were a spring of water,
> and my eyes a fountain of tears,
> so that I might weep day and night

for the slain of my poor people!
O that I had in the desert a traveler's lodging place,
that I might leave my people and go away from them!
For they are all adulterers, a band of traitors. (9:1-2 NRSV)

Perhaps it is Yahweh who speaks here. Perhaps the prophet. Perhaps now, in their grief, they are one. If it is Yahweh who weeps day and night for the people, his grief over their plight is interrupted with the awareness that the plight of the people is a deserved one. Yahweh moves from grief to anger. There is not a more poignant picture in the Old Testament of the suffering God. The God who speaks in Jeremiah 8 is a vulnerable, hurting God who is affected by the faithfulness and faithlessness of the covenant partner to whom God is committed. The people do not "know" him (9:6 NRSV). The intimacy of the relationship has been lost.

Retelling the Story

Jeanne had been sleeping peacefully for almost three hours now. Except for an occasional snore, her breathing was quiet and regular. This had given her son-in-law a chance to read and rest. Though he had dozed briefly, he didn't want to nap for any length of time for fear he would not be able to sleep that night. He knew that he and his wife would both need to stay healthy and rested for these last weeks of her mother's life.

The diagnosis of lung cancer had come just a few days before Christmas—thirteen months ago, months that had been punctuated by chemotherapy and radiation treatments. She had continued to smoke until the treatments had made her so nauseous that she could no longer enjoy either food or cigarettes. Neither warnings from the Surgeon General nor lectures from her younger daughter had discouraged her from smoking. Though she had been restricted to smoking outside the house after her first grandchild was born, she would stand on the porch in her bulky sweater, the smoke encircling her head like a noose in the still, cold night air.

Now it was just past Christmas a little over a year later and the most recent tests were not promising. The oncologists had said she might have eighteen months to two years before the cancer returned in some other organ. The prognosis then would depend on which organ had been invaded and how severely. The cancer returned in the liver and things looked pretty bleak. Now the oncologists talked in terms of weeks rather than months and in single digits at that. There would be no chemotherapy nor radiation this time. The first attempt at a second go-around had almost done her in. "Is there no balm in Gilead?" the prophet had asked. If by balm he meant cure, the answer clearly was no. If his metaphor had intended comfort instead, Was there any comfort physical or otherwise?

Jeanne stirred and attempted to clear her throat. Her son-in-law rose to stand

91

> God is like a king, say the sages, who would take his sons with him to the baths built around a hot spring. One day those sons made the king so angry he vowed never to bring them with him again. Afterward he became lonesome for them and wished he could have them with him. Israel is like the sons who angered the king. Even so, God wishes to have the people nearby. "Oh, how I wish my people were with me, even complaining as they did when I brought them out of Egypt." (*Sefer Ha-Aggadah* 360.11)

by her bedside. He wiped her mouth with a damp washcloth and fed her an installment of her steady diet of ice chips. Her hair had just started to grow out, and it had been brown and curly rather than gray and straight. She had been proud of her new hair until the single treatment in the abandoned second series of chemotherapy took even that. The combination of disease and treatments had meant a continual experience of diminishment. She had lost weight and energy as well as her hair. Even her coffee did not taste the same. Though she tried as hard as she could to enjoy the ordinary experiences of life that had once given her such joy, now they seemed only to tire her out.

"How are you doing?" The question seemed ludicrous given her situation, but he asked it every time she awoke. And she always responded with "Pretty good," which he assumed was as far as she was willing to stretch the truth. Her son-in-law had waited to talk to her about her wishes for the funeral. He hesitated to bring it up too soon but he was afraid of waiting until she could no longer communicate. Then it would be too late, and her family would just have to guess at what she would have wanted.

"Jeanne," he began, "if you don't want to talk about this now just tell me so. I had some questions about your desires for your service . . . " He wasn't sure why he was having this much trouble. He had talked to numerous people about funeral plans before.

"It's OK." Her whispered voice sounded almost like she was comforting him. She continued. "I want it at church and I want you to do it."

"Do you want anyone else involved?"

"No." The answer sounded as if she intended it to end the conversation.

They were silent for several minutes. The son-in-law tried to think of what he was supposed to say next, but nothing came to his mind. He knew there was more information he needed to get but even that seemed inconsequential now. Grief had wiped his mental checklist clean, and the tears he had held in until now had begun to brim over his eyelids. Emotion would have stopped any further questions even if he could have remembered them.

He leaned over and it was as if the words just came pouring out, "I couldn't love you more if you were my own mother."

"I know," she said, and when he leaned back up her eyes were closed. The son-in-law turned and walked to the window. He looked out across the city and thought of all those who suffered alone, isolated by illness or grief or any of the common losses that invade the lives of everyone at one time or another. The God of the brokenhearted, he thought, must be brokenhearted, too.

> "Would that my head were a spring
>   of water,
> my eyes a fountain of tears,
> that I might weep day and night
> for the slain of my people."
>   *(Michael E. Williams)*

JEREMIAH 11:18-20; 15:15-21; 20:7-13

The World Against Me

Jeremiah confesses paranoia, thinking that everyone, including the Lord, is determined to make him suffer.

The Story

It was the LORD who showed me, and so I knew; he opened my eyes to what they were doing. I had been like a pet lamb led trustingly to the slaughter; I did not realize they were hatching plots against me and saying, 'Let us destroy the tree while the sap is in it; let us cut him off from the land of the living, so that his name will be wholly forgotten.'

LORD of Hosts, most righteous judge,
testing the heart and mind,
to you I have committed my cause;
let me see your vengeance on them.

....

LORD, you know;
remember me, and vindicate me,
avenge me on my persecutors.
Be patient with me and do not put
    me off,
see what reproaches I endure for
    your sake.
When I came on your words I
    devoured them;
they were joy and happiness to me,
for you, LORD God of Hosts, have
    named me yours.
I have never kept company with
    revellers,
never made merry with them;
because I felt your hand upon me I
    have sat alone,
for you have filled me with
    indignation.

Why then is my pain unending,
and my wound desperate, past all
    healing?
You are to me like a brook that fails,
whose waters are not to be relied on.
This was the LORD's answer:

If you turn back to me, I shall take
    you back
and you will stand before me.
If you can separate the precious from
    the base,
you will be my spokesman.
This people may turn again to you,
but you are not to turn to them.
To withstand them I shall make you
    strong,
an unscaled wall of bronze.
Though they attack you, they will
    not prevail,
for I am with you to save
and deliver you, says the LORD;
I shall deliver you from the clutches of
    the wicked,
I shall rescue you from the grasp of
    the ruthless.

....

YOU HAVE duped me, LORD,
and I have been your dupe;
you have outwitted me and
    prevailed.
All the day long I have been made a
    laughing-stock;
everyone riricules me.
Whenever I speak I must needs cry
    out,

94

calling, 'Violence!' and 'Assault!'
I am reproached and derided all the
     time
for uttering the word of the LORD.
Whenever I said, 'I shall not call it to
     mind
or speak in his name again,'
then his word became imprisoned
     within me
like a fire burning in my heart.
I was weary with holding it under,
and could endure no more.
For I heard many whispering, 'Terror
     let loose!
Denounce him! Let us denounce
     him.'
All my friends were on the watch for
     a false step,
saying, 'Perhaps he may be tricked;

then we can catch him
and have our revenge on him.'
But the LORD is on my side,
a powerful champion;
therefore my persecutors will stumble
     and fall powerless.
Their abasement will be bitter when
     they fail,
and their dishonour will long be
     remembered.
But, LORD of Hosts, you test the
     righteous
and search the depths of the heart.
To you I have committed my cause;
let me see your vengeance on them.
Sing to the LORD, praise the LORD;
for he rescues the poor
from those who would do them
     wrong.

Comments on the Story

Interspersed in the book of Jeremiah is a series of six personal laments
(11:18–12:6; 15:10-21; 17:14-18; 18:18-23; 20:7-13; 20:14-18), the outpourings of the prophet who becomes overwhelmed by the responsibility and the
consequences of being one of God's spokespersons to Judah. Rarely in
prophetic literature is the private struggle of the prophet accessible to the one
who reads the sayings. In Jeremiah, however, the reader is allowed to enter the
inner recesses of the prophet's heart, mind, and soul; as we become captivated
by his struggles, we are made intensely aware of our own.

The lectionary preserves three of these laments, sometimes called "confessions," and only one in its entirety (20:7-13). While the images used to depict
the prophet's plight vary considerably, the careful reader will notice recurring
motifs in the prophet's struggle. First we will examine the thoughts and feelings of Jeremiah in each of the three texts. Then we will turn to Yahweh's
response.

Jeremiah 11:18-20

"But I was like a gentle lamb led to the slaughter" (v. 19 NRSV). Jeremiah
uses these words to describe what it feels like to be betrayed by those around
him, those who devised schemes against him and were bent on his destruction.
The lamb, on the one hand, is a picture of innocence, the essence of peace. The
lamb is defenseless, dependent on the care of those around him. The lamb is
vulnerable and weak. On the other hand, this simile provides for the reader an

95

image of deceit and violence. The gentle lamb is led to slaughter, unaware of his plight. The lamb is betrayed by one he trusted, and is headed toward death. The simile captures well the plight of Jeremiah who is overwhelmed and perhaps surprised by the evil schemes others have devised against him. The enemy had hoped that Jeremiah would be cut off from the land and that his name would be remembered no longer (v. 19). It would be disastrous for a seventh-century Israelite to lose both land and name.

As storytellers we are not surprised by Jeremiah's subsequent request to Yahweh. We know the story, and we have lived out the story of seeking revenge on the enemy. Jeremiah, being deceived and humiliated by those around him, turns to Yahweh and says "let me see your retribution upon them, for to you I have committed my cause" (v. 20 NRSV). We are uncomfortable with Jeremiah's request—perhaps because it is so vaguely familiar in our own lives. Jeremiah assumes, perhaps, that he is the only one committed, truly committed, to the cause of Yahweh. We also know well this part of the story—the part of the story where the prophet feels no one is as committed as he.

In the edited text, Jeremiah's lament ushers the reader into the larger, more pervasive and related questions of life—why is it that the guilty prosper and the treacherous thrive (12:1)? Jeremiah calls Yahweh to pull them out like sheep for the slaughter (12:3); his hope is that the guilty and the treacherous will, in the end, be the ones to suffer as he has suffered.

Jeremiah 15:15-21

In this second lament Jeremiah brings an intense, direct request to Yahweh. With imperatives the prophet pleads with Yahweh to remember him and deliver him and bring retribution on his persecutors. Yahweh is to blame for the prophet's condition. Briefly the prophet remembers the wonder and joy of his call; the words that Yahweh gave him were a delight (v. 16). But now, it is because of these words that Jeremiah suffers. Having now spoken the word, the prophet finds that he must live life alone. He suffers under the weight of Yahweh's hand; the hand that normally supports and offers care now rests heavily upon his shoulders. The joy and delight of his calling have led to pain that will not cease and to wounds that will not heal. Derision and seclusion are the direct results of being a prophet for Yahweh. The reader is moved by the intensity of Jeremiah's prayer to God.

Jeremiah 20:7-13

Having read the first of Jeremiah's laments, we are not surprised when we read Jeremiah 20:7-13. We know from other laments, and we know from the narrative framework of Jeremiah that describes the hostile encounters he has with the world around him, that the prophetic vocation has dealt him a heavy heart. In chapter 20 Jeremiah again describes his relationships with those around him, those to whom he speaks Yahweh's words. To them he has become a laughingstock. He is mocked, and because the words he speaks are harsh and predict the doom of a people who are destined for violence and destruction, the word is now for him a reproach and a derision.

So why, we ask as readers sympathetic to his plight, why in light of all the humiliation and pain that he experiences, does he continue to speak? It is as if he has no choice. If he decided not to speak in Yahweh's name, there would be something inside him like a burning fire shut up in his bones. No other prophetic text speaks so forcefully about the compulsion to speak; he cannot hold it in. Still, many are watching out for him, eager to denounce him and prevail against him.

As in other laments, Jeremiah asks Yahweh to persecute the enemy. He first speaks with a certainty that Yahweh will be with him. There is no need to ask for Yahweh's help. Yahweh had promised to be with him when he was called. Yahweh would be there. But the lament concludes with these words—"O LORD of hosts, you test the righteous, you see the heart and the mind; let me see your retribution upon them, for to you I have committed my cause" (v. 12 NRSV). The constant thread running throughout the three laments, then, is the persecution that Jeremiah experiences at the hand of those in the community and his pleas to Yahweh to vindicate Jeremiah and his calling.

As friends of Jeremiah, we are curious to know Yahweh's response to these tortured words coming from the one who has been chosen to speak Yahweh's word. In chapter 11, Jeremiah's lament is followed by a separate oracle from Yahweh; it is an oracle against the people of Anathoth. To those who were seeking Jeremiah's life and were admonishing him not to prophesy in Yahweh's name, Yahweh brings a word of punishment—Yahweh will bring disaster upon them. Is this, for the editor of Jeremiah, the answer to Jeremiah's prayer?

In Jeremiah 15, Jeremiah's complaint to Yahweh is followed by explicit words from Yahweh to Jeremiah. Yahweh promises presence to Jeremiah if he continues to utter what is precious and if he continues to be the spokesperson for the Lord. The people will continue to fight against him, but they will not prevail. The promise of deliverance comes encapsulated in three significant Old Testament verbs—Yahweh will *save*; Yahweh will *deliver*; Yahweh will *redeem* the prophet.

In Jeremiah 20, there is no response to the plea of Jeremiah. There is silence, and it is left to the imagination of the storyteller what Yahweh's response would have been.

From the laments of Jeremiah the reader is reminded again and again that being the spokesperson is no easy affair. From the beginning of the story, we know that Jeremiah will often be called to speak *against* the community that he will serve. As we read the narrative and the laments we can see how bringing the word brought Jeremiah into a world of adversity and calamity and often despair. As sympathizers we are bothered by Yahweh's possible commitment to bring destruction to Jeremiah's enemy. Aren't we? Or do we as readers so completely identify with the Jeremiah who struggles to bring a faithful word that we would rejoice in their demise? In the end we are simply left over-whelmed by the recognition that there are strong forces in the world that continually seek to *silence* God's truth. Yet, the call is renewed in another generation, and God continually calls us forth to speak.

Retelling the Story

Excerpt from the journal of Baruch, a scribe:

It is an awful thing to be called into God's service as a mouthpiece for unpopular prophecies. Many people think they want to be the chosen one of God. They think it means being chosen for power and prestige, for glamour and glory, but they are mistaken. I have seen the suffering of the chosen of the Lord and have written the words of lament that came spewing forth from those designated lips. There is no way, though, that I could have cast into words the sobs and moans of hurt and grief that came flowing forth with his bitter tears. It made me glad that I was only the scribe. I hurt for Jeremiah, but Jeremiah hurt for God.

As a boy I raised a lamb, a pet really. I was present at the birth and my father asked me if I wanted to have the lamb as my own. Of course I did. I fed it milk from a skin I shaped to resemble a teat. As my baby drank hungrily, I felt the compassion a mother must feel for her young. When my lambkin wanted to play we romped together and when my baby wanted to sleep we curled up together. We dreamed innocent dreams in which we rollicked in fields where the terrors of the world could not touch us.

The rabbis say that anyone who teaches Torah to the child of a neighbor will be given a seat in the great house of study in paradise. And anyone who teaches Torah to a person of little learning, that teacher will find a lenient ear from God. Even if God had reason to hold a grudge, that grudge will be forgotten for one uneducated child who comes to know Torah. As Jeremiah puts it, "If you can separate the precious from the base, you will be my spokesperson." (*Sefer Ha-Aggadah* 415.129)

My lamb grew in its still-innocent enjoyment of the creation. I grew in the terrible knowledge that one day my friend and I would be separated. I knew the fate of sheep in my father's flock, and for a time I was able to believe that my pet would escape to grow old with me. I begged my father to spare this one small lamb, my own lamb. But that was not to be.

One day my father came to me brandishing a long knife. He told me that the time had come for me to give up childish ways. Not only was my lamb to be slaughtered, but I was the one who would have to put the knife to the throat I held so dear. I felt physically ill at the very thought of it, but I could no more escape my father's decree than could my lamb.

The day came and I knew what I would have to do. At least I could stand behind the lamb as I drew the blade across its throat. It would never need to know that the one who loved it so well was now its executioner. Another of the sheep workers held my lamb as I stepped astride her from behind. She did not struggle, nor did she cry out. The bliss of ignorance was hers. As I held the knife under her neck the other worker quickly jerked her head backward to expose the throat. For one brief horrible moment our eyes met. Those were Isaac's eyes as he looked up at his father with the terrible answer to his question, "Where is the sacrifice?" She knew it was I whom she had trusted who was about to take her life. A sound unlike any I had ever heard a sheep make in all my life was torn from her throat. It said "Betrayer! Betrayer!" Again and again it repeated those same syllables. When I could no longer endure the truth of its cries I drew the knife across her final accusation and all was silent.

Those were the same sounds that came pouring out of our prophet here. His strong accusation of betrayal put me in mind of my lamb. He even used the same figure of speech to describe himself. Perhaps the truth is that we are all lambs, the knife poised at our throats as we blissfully look the other way. We fail, or rather refuse, to recognize the angel of death standing astride of us waiting. Most of us die without ever knowing what hit us, calling the thing fate all along. But to a few of us is given a glance. Our heads are jerked back and for one brief hellish moment we see the one we trusted, knife in hand. We scream betrayal, but it is too late. Our screams only justify our deaths. We must be stopped from telling such terrible truth.

In our own time we all are Isaacs asking the whereabouts of the lamb to be sacrificed. We are all Abrahams answering, "God will provide the sacrifice." But the prophet asks the impertinent question, "But will God then provide justice for the innocent who have been slain? Why do the wicked thrive while the good die?"

> Other sages assert that teaching Torah to another is equal to having assembled that person in the womb and bringing him or her to birth. In fact, to teach Torah is to bring people under the wings of the holy presence of the Holy One. (*Sefer Ha-Aggadah* 415.127)

Then the prophet listens and if no answer readily appears, I can see the dark clouds gather in Jeremiah's imagination. "Why did my mother's womb not become my grave? A curse on the day I was born and on the one who brought the news to my father. Why was I the chosen one, since I was selected for sorrow and sadness. Choose someone else next time for your messages of woe. You look into their eyes and tell them your terrible truths and leave me to lie at peace in my grave."

Sometimes Jeremiah's grief is too much to view. I cannot imagine bearing such sorrow. At times like this I am glad I was only chosen to be a scribe. (Michael E. Williams)

We Thirst

The people plead for salvation, but the Lord says that it is too late.

The Story

Though our sins testify against us,
yet take action, LORD, for your own
name's sake.
Our disloyalties indeed are many;
we have sinned against you.
Hope of Israel, their saviour in time
of trouble,
must you be like a stranger in the
land,
like a traveller breaking his journey
to find a night's lodging?
Must you be like a man suddenly
overcome,
like a warrior powerless to save
himself?
You are in our midst, Lord, and we
bear your name.
Do not forsake us.

The LORD says of this people: They
love to stray from my ways; they wander where they will. Therefore the
LORD has no more pleasure in them;
he remembers their guilt now, and
punishes their sins.
. . . .

Have you spurned Judah utterly?
Do you loathe Zion?
Why have you wounded us past all
healing?
We hoped to prosper, but nothing
went well.
We hoped for respite, but terror
struck.
We acknowledge our wickedness,
the guilt of our forefathers;
LORD, we have sinned against you.
Do not despise the place where your
name dwells
or bring contempt on your glorious
throne.
Remember your covenant with us
and do not make it void.
Can any of the false gods of the
nations give rain?
Or do the heavens of themselves send
showers?
Is it not in you, LORD our God,
that we put our hope?
You alone made all these things.

Comments on the Story

We witness in Jeremiah 14 a careful structure where twice in parallel form
(1) the condition of the community is described, (2) the community laments,
and (3) the community receives a response from Yahweh. In the first sequence,
the description of drought (vv. 1-6) sets the stage for the communal lament
found in Jeremiah 14:7-10. The harsh reality of the catastrophe is brought to
the reader by a continual stream of imagery comparing the predicament of the

people to those who have no water to drink. The nobles send servants for water, but find the cisterns empty. The ground is cracked from lack of rainfall. Farmers lament. Even the mother deer who can find no water forsakes her young. Animals stand on high places and look out to the horizon, but see nothing to eat. The drought extends from the city to the vast regions that surround it. The thirsty ones despair, and they cry out to God.

In the lament (vv. 7-10), the supplication to Yahweh follows confession. The people acknowledge their iniquities, their many apostasies, and their sins. This suggestive range of words that describe the people's "turning away" from Yahweh emphasizes both the breadth and the immensity of their unfaithfulness. They implore Yahweh to save them in spite of what they have done; they ask "why" Yahweh is as a stranger who has turned aside, who is aloof, and who is like a warrior unable to help. Still, they implore (v. 9). They call God to be faithful to the covenant God has made with them. Though they have forsaken Yahweh, they are hopeful that Yahweh will not forsake them forever.

The reader of Jeremiah hears the people pleading to Yahweh and, based on past experience with lamentation, expects to hear a word of hope and salvation from God. But the reader does not find the forgiving, responsive word for which he hoped. Yahweh and the people agree—there has been iniquity and sinfulness (see vv. 7 and 10). Yahweh acknowledges that the people have not been faithful, they have wandered away (v. 10). Yahweh will remember the people's iniquity, and the final word (v. 10) is not a word of restoration, but a word of judgment.

The storyteller is stirred by the plight of the people who hope for their God to save them. And the storyteller is perplexed. Could the people not see that their unfaithfulness to God would bring disaster upon them? Is it integral to the human condition that we not see the consequences of our behavior until those consequences have come crashing down upon us? Can we always expect to be rescued from the situations we have created for ourselves? In Jeremiah 14 the news is not good news; God will not save the people.

Beginning in v. 17, the pattern is repeated; the description of the plight of the community is followed by lament (confession and supplication), and the response of Yahweh to the community. The prophet describes the plight of the community stricken by famine and his own grief at what he sees. The prophet weeps. The reader can sense the plight of the one who struggles to find a place for hope in the midst of great despair. In verses 19-22, the people again beg for Yahweh to remember the covenant made with them. Again they ask "why" Yahweh has not brought healing to them. "Have you completely rejected Judah? Does your heart loathe Zion? Why have you struck us down so that there is no healing for us?" (14:19 NRSV). Again they acknowledge their wickedness, iniquity, and sin (v. 20). Their confessions pour out from them, and they ask Yahweh to remember the covenant. The thirsty people have only one hope—Yahweh their god. There is no idol that can bring rain upon the parched ground, only one God who brings showers from the heavens.

Again the reader is surprised by the response from Yahweh (15:1-4 NRSV). "Though Moses and Samuel stood before me, yet my heart would not turn toward this people. Send them out of my sight, and let them go!" The oracle continues. "Those destined for pestilence, to pestilence, and those destined for the sword, to the sword; those destined for famine, to famine, and those destined for captivity, to captivity." The long awaited word of support and encouragement and hope is not found.

Between the two communal laments in verses 7-10 and 19-22, there is found in the edited text a conversation between Jeremiah and Yahweh. Though this is not found in the lectionary, it does speak powerfully and clearly to the dilemma of the prophet. It also answers the questions that have perplexed the storyteller. Have the people been blind to the disastrous consequences that have inevitably befallen them? Are we, in our human condition, incapable of anticipating the world and life that is ahead if we continue to do as we do and be as we are? The people, Yahweh says, have listened to those who call themselves prophets. They have thought about the future and have searched for peace. But the people have listened to the prophets who assure them that nothing evil will come to them, that no matter how they live life no sword and no famine will come to the land. *The people have listened to the prophet who has spoken only what the people have wanted to hear.* The people have listened to the prophet who has told them their way is the way toward peace, and the people are surprised when war and hunger are upon them. They have listened to the prophet who has a "lying vision" and who is deceived (v. 14).

Now the storyteller understands. It is easy to be seduced by the prophets who would assure us that life as we lead it is life as it is supposed to be. It is easy to be seduced by the prophet who claims to be the voice for God but who speaks no word of obligation or responsibility to God or to the world. We want to believe that is true; but we find out that it is not. And we look around at what we have created, and we cry out to God. And we beg God not to forsake us.

Retelling the Story

"I guess I was the last person you thought would be standing at your door." The man standing at the door must have been in his mid-sixties. His hair was solid white and combed straight back. His pink scalp shone through the furrows between ridges of hair. The red veins stood out against the whites of his eyes as if he hadn't slept for days.

"Do I know you?" Marcia spoke through the gap between the door and doorframe. A sturdy chain assured that the door could not be opened any farther with ease. She didn't want her voice to betray the fear that was creeping up from her stomach toward her throat.

"You do but you may not know that you know me. My name is John Akin, but everybody calls me Jack." He held his eyes directly on her in an attempt to lock his own gaze with hers.

Marcia looked away. "Oh!" she said sharply and took a step backward. *Deep breaths,* she thought to herself. *Don't forget to breathe.* She felt as if a weight lay on her chest and breathing became a conscious pushing against that weight.

"May I come in?" the man's voice sounded distant and hollow, like a voice from a dream. She knew he was waiting for her answer but no words came. For a moment it felt as if the question had not been asked of her at all, but of someone else and she had only overheard it.

"May I come in?" the voice repeated. "I'll understand if you don't want to talk to me."

"No," Marcia heard herself saying. "It's OK. Just a minute." She closed the door and unhooked the chain with mechanical gestures like someone sleepwalking.

When she did open the door it swung wide revealing the rest of the visitor. He was nicely dressed, though his clothes looked old and were somewhat out of fashion. It was obvious that he had dressed for the occasion; he even wore a wrinkled dress shirt and tie. Marcia closed the door behind him and fled into the living room without a motion indicating that he should follow, but he did. As Marcia crossed the room and collapsed onto the sofa like someone exhausted, he stood in front of the chair that sat directly opposite her.

"Aren't you going to invite me to sit down?" the visitor asked in a very matter-of-fact tone.

"Sit," was all the response that Marcia could muster.

"I guess you're wondering why I'm here after all this time," he began. Marcia did not answer nor did she indicate that she had even heard him. "I thought about this a long time before I decided to get in touch with you. You may not have known that I was still alive." At these words Marcia shook her head, still avoiding her visitor's eyes. "You may wish that I weren't still around to show up on your doorstep." Marcia made no response. "I just wanted to see you; how you looked, where you lived, so whenever I thought of you I could imagine what your life was like."

For the first time since the visitor had entered the room Marcia spoke. "There is no way you could imagine what my life has been like." She threw a buzzsaw glare in his direction, meeting his eyes now for the first time. This time he looked away. "I just thought," he stammered, "after all, we are still family."

"No!" Marcia shot back, "We were never family. You saw to that. Why did you come here?"

"I wanted to tell you how sorry I am. I know I hurt you terribly by leaving you and your mother . . . " His voice trailed off into silence.

"Let's get the story straight. First, there is no way on God's earth that you could ever imagine how much you hurt me and Mother. But it wasn't by leaving that you hurt us. That was the biggest favor you could have done for us, to leave. I remember trying to go to sleep as a child wondering just how long it would be before you came stumbling in and you and Mother would wake me with your screaming. Sometimes I wouldn't sleep for the rest of the night. Did you know that? The next morning at breakfast Mother would have a black eye or there would be bruises in the shape of handprints on her neck. She did her best to hide them with makeup, but she couldn't cover everything. If I asked about them she would tell me that she had accidentally run into a doorframe or that the cat had scratched her on the neck. I knew those were lies. I knew who had hurt her and who would have hurt me if I had happened to be within arm's reach. No, you didn't do many things right in this sorry life of yours, but leaving was one of them. Oh, we didn't have much to live on and had to move in with Papa and Gran, but at least we didn't have to be afraid anymore."

When the people were sent into exile, others said of the children of Israel that they were like silver that had been melted down and refined again and again. Silver melted too many times to make different objects finally ceases to be useful and the objects break easily. The exiles felt as if they could be easily broken like overly refined silver. Would there ever be a hope of the people being useful to God again? They did not see how it could ever be so. Jeremiah speaks for them, "Have you spurned Judah utterly? Do you loathe Zion? Why have you wounded us past healing?" (*Sefer Ha-Aggadah* 379.17)

"I kept meaning to send money, but I just never got far enough ahead. I know life wasn't easy for you and your mother. You have to realize, though, that it wasn't easy for me either. I was in the grip of a disease; I know that now. I attend AA meetings every week. I've been sober sixteen months now."

"Good for you. I'm sure Mother would have been pleased to hear that. It's too bad she didn't live to hear your good news." Marcia's voice sounded even more sarcastic than she had intended. "Tell me why it is that if you were the one with the disease, we were the ones who suffered."

"You may not believe this," his voice was still slow and calm, "but I suffered, too. I lost everything. I lost you."

"That was your choice. You were the one who chose to have a series of one-night stands with a bottle of scotch instead of playing with your little girl or coming to her piano recitals or high school graduation. You made that choice."

"You're exactly right. I made the choice to have that first drink, but from then on the disease took over and I didn't really have a choice."

An embarrassed silence sat between them like an obnoxious guest who refuses to leave. If for no other reason than to fill the quiet Marcia asked, "What do you want from me?"

"Your forgiveness."

"I don't have any to give."

"Then let me earn it?"

"You sound like a salesman now." As a child Marcia could remember wanting to have a father. Not a drunk who came home and beat his wife, but a real father, the kind she thought in her childish way that all the other kids had. Now she had a chance to have the father who had rejected her and whom she had rejected back. Now, though, she wasn't so sure she wanted any father at all. "I don't know. I don't even know you for God's sake. I didn't even recognize you after all these years. I'll have to think it over. Come back next Tuesday."
(Michael E. Williams)

Curse and Blessing

In the midst of drought, the prophet insists that the people trust in the Lord, and not in themselves.

The Story

These are the words of the LORD:

A curse on anyone who trusts in mortals
and leans for support on human kind,
while his heart is far from the Lord!
He will be like a juniper in the steppeland;
when good comes he is unaware of it.
He will live among the rocks in the wilderness,
in a salt, uninhabited land.

Blessed is anyone who trusts in the LORD,
and rests his confidence on him.
He will be like a tree planted by the waterside,
that sends out its roots along a stream.
When the heat comes it has nothing to fear;
its foliage stays green.
Without care in a year of drought,
it does not fail to bear fruit.

Comments on the Story

The poem seems strangely out of place and disturbs the fiery staccato of the words of Jeremiah fired against the people of Judah who have forsaken their covenant with Yahweh. Couched in the wonderful world of metaphor, the words of warning take on a gentler, quieter form. Yet, for the careful reader, the message of Jeremiah is still urgently present—there is only one place where trust should rest. Trust only in Yahweh.

In this first of three wisdom sayings (vv. 5-8; 9-10; 11) the author has drawn upon the metaphor of water to portray the life-giving God. Contrast is used in superb fashion to draw the tight distinction between the one who trusts in humanity and the one who trusts in God. The stark contrast is made more graphic by the introductory words "cursed" (v. 5) and "blessed" (v. 7). This is not simply a picture of two ways to live. These are descriptions of life and death. The poet begins with the "bad news."

Cursed is the one who trusts in mortals. The curiosity of the storyteller is piqued. Is one not to trust in the companion, the neighbor, or the friend? That is not the point. Cursed is the one who sees flesh as strength and whose heart has turned away from Yahweh (v. 5); the point becomes clear. Cursed is the one who trusts only in what one can see. The author, writing in a dry land where water often becomes the key between life and death, depicts this one who trusts in mortals as the shrub in the desert. Either the shrub never receives relief or it does not see it when it comes (v. 6). Regardless, the shrub is rooted in a dry, cracked land. It is an uninhabited land because nothing can survive there.

Blessed, however, are those who trust in Yahweh. Unlike the cursed ones doomed to die in the unfertile land, these are like the tree planted by water. These are like the tree rooted by the stream (v. 8). The tree, actively participating in its future, sends out its roots; it reaches for the life-giving water. The verb form here depicts rigor and intensity as the tree searches out its nourishment.

Interestingly, the tree that has thrust its roots to the water's edge is free from fear and from anxiety. It never ceases to be fertile.

The storyteller is captivated by this contrast. The cursed one is obviously doomed to die; the blessed one will live abundantly. But it is the similarity between the cursed and the blessed ones that provides the foundation for the story. *Both* experience the drought. *Both* experience the seasons when the rain does not flow from the heavens; *both* experience the overwhelming heat. The first does not even see relief when it comes. The second does not fear and is not anxious. It does not cease bearing fruit. The difference is *not* in the experiences life brings. The difference is where one is planted.

In one sense the poem speaks to the decisions that the people of Judah, who decide daily where to place trust, have faced and will continue to face. In another sense, the poem speaks in a poignant way to the life story of the prophet, who has continually received resistance and vengeance from the community who did not want to hear Yahweh's word. Daily, he too had to decide where he should place his trust—in mortals and in their responses to him? Is that what he should trust? Or in Yahweh who has promised to be with him as he delivers the tough, but ultimately lifesaving, words?

Bound within its lyrics the songwriter speaks to the people of Judah and to himself and to us of the choices we have as we go about life. The choice involves trust and heart and where we place them. Whether or not we survive the drought will depend on that decision, and according to the poet, on that decision alone.

Retelling the Story

The Ballad of the Heart at Ease

Who is wise my child, my child?
Who is wise, my child?

108

Those who live in a Godly style
Who never curse nor yet revile
But bless with words that heal, my
　　child.
But bless with words that heal.

Who is good, my son, my son?
Who is good, my son?
Those who trust in God, the One
Who trust from rise 'til set of sun
Then trust the whole night, too, my
　　son.
Then trust the whole night, too.

Who is strong, my daughter, my
　　daughter?
Who is strong, my daughter?
Those who behave and speak as they
　　oughtta
Who are like trees by rivers of water
Bearing fruit in the heat and the
　　drought, my daughter.
Who bear fruit in the heat and the
　　drought.

When shall my heart be at ease, my
　　God?
When shall my heart be at ease?
When all of your words and your
　　deeds shall me please.
When by every river and by all my
　　seas
My people shall stand like a nation
　　of trees.
Then shall your heart be at ease, my
　　Child.
Then shall your heart be at ease.
(Michael E. Williams)

Those who take charity but really don't need it will live to need it say the sages. And those who refuse charity when they really could use it will live to have enough to share with others. That is what Jeremiah means when he says, "Blessed is anyone who trusts in the Lord." (*Sefer Ha-Aggadah* 674.318)

A rabbi returning home heard cries for help coming from his hometown. Instead of allowing panic to take over, he said in his own heart that the cries must not be from members of his family. Such was his trust in God. (*Sefer Ha-Aggadah* 206.19)

It Is No Use

Jeremiah watches a potter remake a pot.

The Story

THESE are the words which came to Jeremiah from the LORD: Go down now to the potter's house, and there I shall tell you what I have to say. I went down to the potter's house, where I found him working at the wheel. Now and then a vessel he was making from the clay would be spoilt in his hands, and he would remould it into another vessel to his liking.

Then the word of the LORD came to me: Israel, can I not deal with you as this potter deals with his clay? says the LORD. House of Israel, you are clay in my hands like the clay in his. At any moment I may threaten to uproot a nation or a kingdom, to pull it down and destroy it. But if the nation which I have threatened turns back from its wicked ways, then I shall think again about the disaster I had in mind for it. At another moment I may announce that I shall build or plant a nation or a kingdom. But if it does evil in my sight by disobeying me, I shall think again about the good I had in mind for it.

Go now and tell the people of Judah and the citizens of Jerusalem that these are the words of the LORD: I am framing disaster for you and perfecting my designs against you. Turn back, every one of you, from his evil conduct; mend your ways and your actions. But they will answer, 'Things are past hope. We must stick to our own plans, and each of us follow the promptings of his wicked and stubborn heart.'

Comments on the Story

Chapter 18 recounts another symbolic act in the book of Jeremiah, another illustration of an incident in the prophet's life when an ordinary object or an ordinary event yields new insight and understanding, a word from Yahweh.

Jeremiah is told to go to the potter's house; his visit there is outlined in verses 1-4. He must wonder why it is he has been sent there. He must wonder what word will confront him. He watches the potter working at the wheel; there is nothing particularly unusual in the potter's work. That which the potter is creating is flawed; the potter reworks the clay until the vessel seems good to him.

Jeremiah observes and waits and the word comes as promised. It is a word for the house of Israel. Yahweh recounts that like the clay in the potter's hands, so Israel is in the hands of Yahweh. The lessons drawn from the experience of

110

watching the potter are ambiguous—like all images this one is suggestive of many possible interpretations. "Can I not do with you, O house of Israel, just as the potter has done?" Yahweh asks. Does Yahweh mean that Yahweh has power and control over the people as the potter has over the clay? Can Yahweh discard the clay that seems to be resistant to the potter's purpose? The reader is intrigued, or perhaps bothered, by the images of power and control.

But the reader also senses a hint, a possibility of another dynamic. It is a more hopeful one. Just as the potter hopes to fashion the useful vessel, so Yahweh *longs* for the people of Israel to listen to Yahweh's voice and to turn from evil. The potter works and reworks the clay until the appropriate vessel is made. Power is tempered by patience. In the end, how the people respond to Yahweh will determine the response of Yahweh to them. If the nation that is to be destroyed by Yahweh repents, Yahweh will turn from bringing disaster to it. And if the nation that Yahweh is building turns away, Yahweh will turn away from it. When the people turn, Yahweh turns. Is this good news? Yes! The people can control their future.

The storyteller is delighted with these first ten verses in the eighteenth chapter of Jeremiah. In the midst of the accusations hurled against the people, there seems to be within the narrative a glimmer of hope. The people can choose to turn toward Yahweh and Yahweh in turn will turn toward them (v. 8). The destruction that had seemed so inevitable will not then come to pass. As readers we sigh in relief. All will be well.

The last word, however, is not so comforting. Yahweh speaks to Jeremiah, "Now, therefore, say to the people of Judah and the inhabitants of Jerusalem: Thus says the LORD: Look, I am a potter shaping evil against you and devising a plan against you. Turn now, all of you from your evil way, and amend your ways and your doings" (18:11 NRSV). Our hopes are that in this final hour, as devastation comes dangerously near, the people will know that this may be their final chance. What will they do? Surely they will come closer to Yahweh. . . .

They do not. The people choose to follow their own way, a different way (v. 12). We wonder why, and we are perplexed. Yahweh has allowed for the possibility of change in the hearts of Yahweh's people. But the people themselves do not. "It is no use!" the people say; all their hope and desire for repentance seems to be gone. And we wonder, Do they not know that there is always the possibility for change? Or have they chosen death for so long that they now do not know how to choose life?

Retelling the Story

Excerpt from the journal of Baruch, a scribe:

One morning I arrived at work to find the prophet dressed as if to leave for a journey. I asked him where he was going and how long he would be away. "Not

I, my friend," he replied looking at me with that intense gaze of his. You know I never was quite sure whether he was looking at me or through me. "We are going to a place God has shown me. A place where the future of this people of ours will be revealed. We are going to the potter's house and we will observe the artist at work in expectation of seeing God's hand there as well. Come along."

So I gathered up my instruments and followed. The prophet always walked with an urgency that made him difficult to keep up with. It seemed to me as if he were hurling himself headlong into God's future, never really knowing for sure what he would encounter there. Perhaps he trusted the One who called him into that future and this trust drove away all fear. Or perhaps he simply had little regard for his own well-being. I never could tell which impulse drove him, and speaking truthfully, it always made me more than a little nervous.

In spite of my natural concern for my own well-being, I followed. I could see no harm that could come to us in the house of a potter. The prophet entered without knocking, which was his usual practice when in this state of urgency. The potter looked a bit startled at first but soon asked us to sit. He worked with only clay and a bit of water as his materials. His hands and the wheel were his tools. We observed as he took a lump of this clay, and as it turned on the wheel he slowly worked it until it began to take shape with a shallow bowl-shaped recess at its center. Then wetting his hand again he placed his fingers in the bowl part and his thumbs on the outside. Almost as if by magic he raised the sides of the bowl up away from the wheel. Just then as the sides were rising, the bowl went lopsided, one part leaning akimbo away from the rest. As it turned on the wheel it put me in mind of someone limping, dipping more to one side than the other as he walks.

This course of events didn't seem to disturb the potter greatly. He simply stopped the wheel and pounded the clay back into a lump, then began turning the wheel again. He proceeded through the same process as before and a second time something went amiss. This time one side of the pot was noticeably thicker than the other. A second time the potter beat on the clay until it was a lumpish mass. "How many times will you have to rework the pot before you decide it's hopeless and throw it away?" I inquired.

"In the first place you didn't see the first three times I tried to raise a pot from this particular lump before you came in. And as for throwing it away, I

Some of the sages suggest that the making of a pot bears similarities to giving birth. Just as a potter's wheel sits between the potter's legs and on it the pot is formed, so the child comes from between his mother's legs. Thus the creative process in art is in some respects similar to the creation of new life. Perhaps it also suggests that God takes a motherly care of this peculiar work of art, this child of God, Israel. (*Exodus Rabbah* 1.14) wouldn't dream of doing such a thing. Good clay is not a thing to waste. I'll just keep working with it until I discover the vessel that is hidden inside. If I keep at it that vessel will emerge sooner or later. You don't waste good clay. Remember that, young man."

Finally, following several additional attempts the potter raised a fine-looking piece. I noted that this final pot was very different from the first I had seen him try, as if there was some form there living inside that lump of clay just waiting to be discovered by the hands of a skillful artist. "I have seen what I came to see," the prophet blurted out and with an abrupt farewell rose to leave. I thanked the potter for his time and followed.

When we arrived back at the prophet's house he went into the cool darkness of his room and left me to wait on the word of the Lord that would come to him and that he would then instruct me to write. As he waited on the word I napped. My sleep was interrupted by dreams in which disks whirled like the potter's wheel making me dizzy, and in which I was forced to repeat activities that never seemed to come to any productive conclusion.

Finally, late in the afternoon, the prophet emerged and said to write this: "I am the potter and you are the clay, O Israel. Can I not treat you like the potter does the clay when the pot turns out all wrong? Do you think I will not pound you into a lump again and again if you continue to defy me? I can raise up nations like pots and I can beat them down again. You know this is no boast. You know from your own history that what I say is true. But if a nation turns back to me, I will remember what a beautiful pot is hidden within the cloak of its sinfulness. If a nation continues to turn against me, I will pound it into a lump and may forget the vessel it was intended to be.

"Now go to my people and tell them that they must turn back from the evil they do one another. Tell them they must learn again to be the vessel I intended

There was an important and highly respected physician whose son fell into the company of a quack who sold fraudulent cures under the name "Father John's Tonics." When the true physician heard that his son was referring to the fraud as "Father John," he was hurt and angry. Some time later the young man became quite ill and called for his father to come cure him. His father came and gave the boy what he needed to be brought back to health, but he was still distressed by his son's behavior. The doctor asked his son, "Why is it that when you are well you call someone else 'father.' When you get truly sick you call me 'father' again." This is the way God feels when the people worship idols during the good times and only turn to the true God when things are in crisis. Even when Jeremiah calls God "father," God is still suspicious. (*Exodus Rabbah* 46.4) them to be from the first. If they do this I will work with them and raise them up. But if they think things are past hope, that they cannot rely on me but turn back to their evil devices, then I will pound them into a mass of clay that has no recognizable shape and is nothing more than a lump. Tell them this, O prophet." The prophet fell exhausted on the floor. I lifted him up and put him on his pallet to sleep.

I knew that tomorrow he would be proclaiming in the streets what he had just dictated to me. I knew as well that the people would receive such words, if at all, as excuses for their hopelessness. As I walked home I began to wonder if there was something missing from the prophet's message. Hadn't the potter said after all that you don't waste good clay? (Michael E. Williams)

Like a Good Shepherd, Lead

The prophet anticipates a homecoming, when the nation would be restored by the Lord, in spite of shepherds and prophets who deceive the people.

The Story

Woe betide the shepherds who let the sheep of my flock scatter and be lost! says the LORD. Therefore these are the words of the LORD the God of Israel to the shepherds who tend my people: You have scattered and dispersed my flock. You have not watched over them; but I am watching you to punish you for your misdeeds, says the LORD. I myself shall gather the remnant of my sheep from all the lands to which I have dispersed them. I shall bring them back to their homes, and they will be fruitful and increase. I shall appoint shepherds who will tend them, so that never again will they know fear or dismay or punishment. This is the word of the LORD.

The days are coming, says the LORD, when I shall make a righteous
　Branch spring from David's line,
a king who will rule wisely,
maintaining justice and right in the
　land.
In his days Judah will be kept safe,
and Israel will live undisturbed.
This will be the name to be given to
　him:
The LORD our Righteousness.

Therefore the time is coming, says the LORD, when people will no longer swear 'by the life of the LORD who brought the Israelites up from Egypt'; instead they will swear 'by the life of the LORD who brought the descendants of the Israelites back from a northern land and from all the lands to which he had dispersed them'; and they will live on their own soil.

....

Am I a God near at hand only, not a
　God when far away?
Can anyone hide in some secret place
　and I not see him?
Do I not fill heaven and earth?
This is the word of the LORD.

I have heard what the prophets say, the prophets who speak lies in my name; they cry, 'I have had a dream, I have had a dream!' How much longer will these prophets be minded to prophesy lies and give voice to their own inventions? By these dreams which they tell one another they think they will make my people forget my name, just as their fathers forgot my name for the name of Baal. If a prophet has a dream, let him tell his dream; if he has my word, let him speak my word faithfully. Chaff and grain are quite distinct, says the LORD. Are not my words like fire, says the Lord; are they not like a hammer that shatters rock? Therefore I am against those prophets, the impostors who steal my words from the others, says the LORD. I am against those prophets, says the LORD, who concoct words of their own and then say, 'This is his word,' I am against those prophets, says the LORD, who deal in false dreams and relate them to mislead my people with wild and reckless falsehoods. It was not I who sent them or commissioned them, and they will do this people no good service. This is the word of the LORD.

....

The days are coming, says the LORD, when I shall bestow on Israel and Judah all the blessings I have promised them. In those days, at that time, I shall make a righteous Branch spring from David's line; he will maintain law and justice in the land. In those days Judah will be kept safe and Jerusalem will live undisturbed. This will be the name given to him: the LORD our Righteousness.

Comments on the Story

Jeremiah 23:1-8 is divided into three smaller units, each bringing a word of hope to Yahweh's people. In verses 1-4, through a "woe" oracle, the prophet brings a challenging word to the shepherds of Israel. While oft times in the Hebrew scriptures the shepherd is the symbol for Israel's king, here the referent is left ambiguous and the reader is invited to visualize any of the nation's political and religious leaders who have responsibility for leading and guiding the community. The word to the shepherds is a word of admonition. The shepherds have scattered the flock, driven them away and have not attended to them (v. 2).

Yahweh will now "attend" to those who have not "attended" to the community. In contrast to the shepherds who have scattered the flock, Yahweh will gather them (v. 3); the bringing of the people back to the land is one of many portraits painted in the Old Testament of the grand homecoming. The storyteller is interested in this portrait of the return painted by the prophet. The people who return will no longer be afraid or dismayed. "Nor shall any be missing" (v. 4 NRSV). With this simple phrase the prophetic word speaks to the ultimate conception of community. *All* are there; *none* is missing.

In the second oracle (vv. 5-6), the righteous Branch of David's line is restored to power. From its inception, this line of rulers was one that was to bring justice and righteousness to the community. As history sadly recounts, this was not always the case. But now, the prophet proclaims for Yahweh, the new rulers will bring salvation to Judah and safety to Israel. This oracle is much like the one found in Jeremiah 33:14-16 where, with similar wording, the promise of the new Branch is brought forth. This short oracle, brought together in a collection (vv. 14-26) of messianic prophecies, assures the community that Yahweh will fulfill the "good word" once brought to Israel and Judah. While the similarities between 23:5-6 and 33:14-16 are stunning, so are the differences. In chapter 33, the good news is brought to Judah and Jerusalem (not Israel) and it is not the ruler but the city that is given a new name—"Yahweh is our righteousness."

While the concept of God's good inclination toward the dynasty and family of David is not prominent in Jeremiah, it is part of Israel's stock of promises and is probably included here as one of the many ways in which Israel voices its hope. The contrast between the failure of the shepherds who have scattered the flock (23:1-4) and the promise of a restored line of rulers who will bring justice and righteousness (23:5-6) is striking. The juxtaposition reminds the storyteller of the importance of those who lead—they can bring great good . . . or great harm to the communities they serve.

The final unit in 23:7-8 brings the chorus to a grand finale. The restoration that will come from the hand of Yahweh will supplant the deliverance brought to the Israelites when they were brought up out of Egypt. The people will now be able to speak of their own deliverance from the land of the north and all the lands to which they have been dispersed. The storyteller is captivated by the difference between "God delivered our ancestors" and "God has delivered us." There is a radical difference between assertions about that which God *has done* and that which God *is doing*.

*   *   *

God is everywhere; God is both nearby and far away; God fills heaven and earth. With this assertion Jeremiah 23:23-32 begins. And because God is everywhere God has heard the prophets—prophets who have lied in God's name. Irony is present in the words of the lying prophet who says "I have dreamed! I have dreamed!" The irony is that the lying prophet has, in some sense, spoken truth. The prophet speaks of what he *alone* has dreamed. He prophesies out of his own heart, she prophesies with her own words. But the true prophet for Yahweh speaks Yahweh's word (v. 28). The two similes used to describe Yahweh's word are powerfully effective. The storyteller is invited to ask—When is Yahweh's word like fire?

And when is Yahweh's word like a hammer that breaks rock (v. 29)? These fascinating descriptions of the word are followed by a three-fold admonition (vv. 30-32). Emphatically the people are reminded that Yahweh is against the prophet who would steal from another, who would claim to speak a word from Yahweh when only speaking his own, or who would prophesy lying dreams and lead the people astray.

Again, the important function of those who lead in the community is stressed. Yahweh speaks about those whose prophecy is not true; those prophets who have no integrity. They are not sent by Yahweh. While there is clearly a difference between the prophet who would speak for Yahweh and the one who would not, the ambiguous nature of prophecy for the community remains. Even when searching for the true and authentic word, one can be deceived. How does one know the true word when it is heard? And how does one know if one is speaking a true word?

Retelling the Story

> One of the Roman nobility argued with one of the sages that the god she worshiped was greater than the God of Israel. The argument ran this way: When Moses heard the God of Israel from the burning bush he only hid his face, but when he saw the serpent he ran. This, it seemed to the Roman, proved that the serpent was the more powerful of the two. The rabbi proposed another interpretation. Where could Moses have run to escape the God who created all that is and sees all that is? But to escape the Roman god he only needed to run a few steps and the snake was powerless. (*Sefer Ha-Aggadah* 504.12)

Mother acts as if I am the only boy who ever got to talking and lost track of the time. The truth is that I frequently become preoccupied with the things I think about. And I so rarely have someone else to talk with about the things that occupy my mind. My hometown is such a small place. All the people here ever want to talk about is money or politics, or the things they say in whispered voices that I am not supposed to hear. I am sure they think that I seem strange, since my interests don't go in those directions. Those who don't particularly like me call me names I can't repeat here. Those who do like me tell me I will grow up to be a teacher. I hope they are right.

My mother is overly protective, if you ask me. She seems to have the idea that I have been set apart by God for some great purpose. What that great purpose might be I do not know and she won't tell. Maybe she doesn't even know. She just worries about me even more than most mothers worry, all because of the one time I went exploring on my own.

After all, I wasn't lost. She just wasn't looking in the right places. I was fine, though, the whole time. This is how it happened. We made our yearly trip to the big city. The whole family came along, including aunts, uncles, cousins, and a few friends too. Once in the city we ran from one place to the next, often having to push our way through the crowds of people who clogged the narrow streets. My favorite place was the Temple. It is strange for a small-town boy from up-country to say, but I felt right at home there. After all the religious ceremonies were finished the teachers would gather and discuss the Scriptures. That was my favorite part. I could sit and listen to their stories and sayings for hours.

In fact that is exactly what I did. I sat and listened for many days and never got tired of it. Every now and then I would ask a question. Other than those few interruptions I sat quietly and soaked in their conversation. After some time, I really don't know for sure how long, the teachers began to talk about the prophet Jeremiah. They began to speak of the shepherd who scattered the flock. Only wicked or foolish shepherds would dream of scattering the sheep in their care. They might never get them gathered together again. The teachers insisted that the prophet was not talking about real shepherds. Rather it was the leaders of our people who were the wicked or foolish shepherds. And sure enough after the people were scattered to Babylon those shepherds were powerless to bring them back together again.

> No one can totally hide his deeds, since God can see everywhere. Anyone who hides to study Torah will be seen by others in the way that that person goes about everyday life. Conversely, those who hide to deceive and do evil will be known by the way they live their lives, as well. Perhaps it is not only God who sees the effects of the things we do in secret. (*Sefer Ha-Aggadah* 709.219)

Then in quieter tones they began to speak of our own leaders, especially the one who calls himself King of the Jews. These too are shepherds who scatter their flocks for their own political gain. It is always easier to weep over the wicked than it is to seek out the righteous. I asked them about the good shepherd. What would a good shepherd act like? They told me that the good shepherd would be a king like David, a soldier like Joshua, and a sage like Solomon. Then something very odd took place, something that had never happened before—at least it had never happened to me. One of the teachers asked me what I thought the good shepherd would be like.

I told them that the good shepherd, like David, would face the lion or the bear or the Philistine giant and if necessary would lay down life and limb for the sheep. Like Joshua, the good shepherd would fight only as God directed, using trumpets or words as weapons. And just as Solomon's wisdom was used to bring the people together, the good shepherd would make sure that not a single sheep was lost. After all, hadn't the prophet said "Nor shall any be missing"? I had the idea that if anyone really wanted to be a good shepherd, that person would see that not a soul was lost, that the family would all be gathered around the table.

It was just at that time, as I was talking and all the teachers were listening that my mother burst upon the scene acting like a typical mother. She told me how worried she and Joseph had been when they discovered that I was not with the rest of the family on the way home. She said they had been searching the city for three days. She wept and she laughed and she scolded. When she finished I said something that to this day I am not sure why I said. I just said the first thing that came to mind. I asked her, "Didn't you know I would be in my father's house?"

This threw her off-balance for a moment, since I clearly wasn't in the house that my family called home. To tell you the truth it didn't really make a lot of sense to me at the time. Except that I did feel at home there in the Temple talking with the teachers. In any case my mother hugged me and we all went home. She didn't say anything more about my getting lost and then being found. But I thought about it a lot. In truth I realized it was my mother who would have laid down her life to save mine. She would have employed all the weapons in a woman's arsenal to protect me. She was the one who came looking for the lost sheep, to make sure that none should be missing. Now I carry a vivid picture of the good shepherd in my mind; it is my mother barging into the temple to reclaim her lamb. *(Michael E. Williams)*

The sages observe that a stick standing by itself will not burst into flame of its own accord. Though God has compared the divine word to fire, it will not catch flame in one who studies alone. One catches that fire from others, thus study must be done in company with others. (*Sefer Ha-Aggadah* 428.260)

A Cacophony of Voices

*Dueling prophets vie for attention as the people wonder who is telling
the truth, which is a matter of life and death.*

The Story

AT the beginning of the reign of
Jehoiakim son of Josiah, king of
Judah, this word came from the LORD:
These are the words of the LORD: Stand
in the court of the LORD's house and
speak to the inhabitants of all the towns
of Judah who come to worship there. Tell
them everything that I charge you to say
to them; do not cut it short by one word.
Perhaps they may listen, and everyone
may turn back from evil ways. If they do,
I shall relent, and give up my plan to
bring disaster on them for their evil
deeds. Say to them: These are the words
of the LORD: If you do not obey me, if you
do not live according to the law I have
set before you, and listen to the words of
my servants the prophets, whom again
and again I have been sending to you,
though you have never listened to them,
then I shall do to this house as I did to
Shiloh, and make this city an object of
cursing to all nations on earth.

The priests, the prophets, and all
the people heard Jeremiah say this in
the LORD's house and, when he came
to the end of what the LORD had
charged him to say to them, the
priests and prophets and all the people seized him and threatened him
with death. 'Why', they demanded, 'do
you prophesy in the LORD's name that
this house will become like Shiloh and
this city an uninhabited ruin?' The
people all crowded round Jeremiah in
the LORD's house. When the chief officers of Judah heard what was happening, they went up from the royal
palace to the LORD's house and took
their places there at the entrance of
the New Gate.

The priests and the prophets said to
the officers and all the people, 'This
man deserves to be condemned to
death, because he has prophesied
against this city, as you yourselves have
heard.' Then Jeremiah said to all the
officers and people, 'The LORD it was
who sent me to prophesy against this
house and this city all the things you
have heard. Now, if you mend your
ways and your actions and obey the
LORD your God, he may relent and
revoke the disaster which he has pronounced against you. But here I am in
your hands; do with me whatever you
think right and proper. Only you may
be certain that, if you put me to death,
you and this city and those who live in
it will be guilty of murdering an innocent man; for truly it was the LORD who
sent me to you to say all this to you.'

The officers and all the people then
said to the priests and the prophets,
'This man ought not to be condemned
to death, for he has spoken to us in
the name of the LORD our God.' Some
of the elders of the land also stood up
and said to the whole assembled people, 'In the time of King Hezekiah of

121

Judah, Micah of Moresheth was prophesying and said to all the people of Judah: "These are the words of the LORD of Hosts:

Zion will become a ploughed field,
Jerusalem a heap of ruins,
and the temple hill rough heath."

'Did King Hezekiah and all Judah put him to death? Did not the king show reverence for the LORD and seek to placate him, so that the Lord relented and revoked the disaster which he had pronounced on them? But we are on the point of inflicting great disaster on ourselves.'

There was another man too who prophesied in the name of the LORD: Uriah son of Shemaiah, from Kiriath-jearim. He prophesied against this city and this land, just as Jeremiah had done. King Jehoiakim with his body-guard and all his officers heard what he said and sought to put him to death. On hearing of this, Uriah fled in fear to Egypt. King Jehoiakim dispatched Elnathan son of Akbor with some others to fetch Uriah from Egypt. When they brought him to the king, he had him put to the sword and his body flung into the burial-place of the common people. But Ahikam son of Shaphan used his influence on Jeremiah's behalf to save him from death at the hands of the people.

....

The prophet Jeremiah gave this reply to Hananiah the prophet in the presence of the priests and all the people standing there in the LORD's house: 'May it be so! May the LORD indeed do this: may he fulfil all that you have prophesied, by bringing back the furnishings of the LORD's house together with all the exiles from Babylon to this place! Only hear what I have to say to you and to all the people: The prophets who preceded you and me from earliest times have foretold war, famine, and pestilence for many lands and for great kingdoms. If a prophet foretells prosperity, it will be known that the LORD has sent him only when his words come true.'

Then the prophet Hananiah took the yoke from the neck of the prophet Jeremiah and broke it, announcing to all the people, 'These are the words of the LORD: So shall I break the yoke of King Nebuchadnezzar of Babylon; I shall break it off the necks of all nations within two years.' Then the prophet Jeremiah went his way.

....

Jeremiah sent a letter from Jerusalem to the elders who were left among the exiles, to the priests, prophets, and all the people whom Nebuchadnezzar had deported from Jerusalem to Babylon. . . .

These are the words of the LORD of Hosts the God of Israel: To all the exiles whom I deported from Jerusalem to Babylon: Build houses and live in them; plant gardens and eat the produce; marry wives and rear families; choose wives for your sons and give your daughters to husbands, so that they may bear sons and daughters. Increase there and do not dwindle away. Seek the welfare of any city to which I have exiled you, and pray to the LORD for it; on its welfare your welfare will depend. For these are the words of the LORD of Hosts the God of Israel: Do not be deceived by the prophets and diviners among you, and pay no attention to the women whom you set to dream dreams. They prophesy falsely to you in my name; I did not send them. This is the word of the LORD.

Comments on the Story

Jeremiah 26–29 is an extended narrative that recounts for the reader an edited conversation between the prophets and Yahweh. Chapter 26:1 sets the historical context for the first interchange—it occurs at the beginning of the reign of King Jehoakim in Judah. The first conversation makes it clear that the issue at hand is the "word." The "word" comes Yahweh (v. 1); Jeremiah is commanded to speak all of the "words" to Judah that he has heard (v. 2). That *all* is to be related to the community is reemphasized in the rejoinder: "do not hold back a 'word.'" The consequences for the community that chooses not to hear the "words" are laid out clearly for the community (v. 6).

The task for Jeremiah is put forth clearly; the implications for the community are equally explicit. And yet, there are implied in these words from Yahweh the ambiguity and dubious nature of the task assigned to the prophet. Yahweh knows that the prophet may be tempted to share only part of the message received. Equally clear is the reality that the community may or may not choose to listen. The stage is set then for the series of events to follow. Jeremiah speaks, and as readers we have been prepared for the unsettling responses he receives. Because he has spoken harsh words against the city, some call for his death (26:8). Jeremiah, unrelenting, speaks again (vv. 12-15). And the officials and the people realize that in Jeremiah's words there is a word from Yahweh (v. 16).

The chapter comes to a close with what appears to be an inserted story about the prophet Uriah who had also once prophesied harsh words to the King Jehoiakim. Uriah died at the king's hand. We are subtly reminded about the power of the spoken "word." The words of Uriah were so frightening to the king that the one who spoke them had to die. We are reminded how difficult it is to hear a word we *do not* want to hear. Jeremiah, however, unlike Uriah lives and the story goes on.

Woven through the remaining segments of the unit (vv. 27-29) are various reminders to the community that they may encounter words—words from prophets that are not words from Yahweh. The first caution comes in 27:14 where the people are admonished not to listen to the words of prophets who tell them not to serve the king of Babylon for they are prophesying lies. Yahweh states clearly, "I have not sent them. . . . " This cautionary word is then demonstrated in the recounting of a story—the story of Jeremiah and the "false" prophet Hananiah. The reader is allowed to experience the tense encounter between them and realizes that to hear the word of Yahweh may not be as simple and uncomplicated as first sounds. The truth expressed in chapters 27-29 is this: We are surrounded by a cacophony of voices speaking words, words themselves that claim to be truth. And we are called to make decisions about the truth claims they present to us. According to the Jeremianic narrative, Hananiah, the false prophet, dies in the same year he spoke the congenial, but false, prophecy to the people. The editor wants us to understand the enormous ramifications for those who claim to speak the word of the Lord, but who, in reality, speak only words the community wants to hear. Hananiah speaks lies; Hananiah dies. And yet we know from our own life experience that the announcement about Hananiah's death makes the complex far too simple. We are often called to decide who is speaking truth with few such clear signs to guide us.

At the conclusion of this four-chapter segment (chapter 29), Jeremiah sends a letter, a word to the community then exiled in Babylon. It is a letter in which he relays the word from Yahweh. In exile, the community is to build houses and live in them—plant gardens, have children, and seek the welfare of the cities where they live. To seek the welfare of the city is to seek their own welfare (v. 7).

We know the end to the larger story, as did the one who compiled these narratives for us. We know that Jeremiah spoke truth; that the return of the Israelites from captivity would not take place that year or the next, not even in the same generation. Again that is not the word the people would have wanted to hear. They would be barraged with words from other prophets who would deliver to them the easy message, the comforting message—"soon you will go home." As readers we are encouraged to hope for them that they can hear the "true" word. But from our own life experience we know how difficult it is to hear the words that seem to come to us from every direction and to discern which of them is true. We know how difficult it is to believe the word we do not want to hear. The storyteller will be able to bring that reality to life.

Retelling the Story

Hananiah's Lament

I had only wanted to say a good word,
a word of hope to those
whose lives were frail as breath,
as fragile as a strand of spider web.

The people had once again
seen their dreams dissolve in a stream of time.
Their history careened once more
toward the seemingly inevitable abyss.

There has been too much of this,
my heart cried out in grief, surely God
will intervene, will save the people
from ourselves at last.

What mother would sell her son
into slavery for laziness?
What father would give his daughter
to an enemy to be raped for talking back?

What kind of deity would defile, destroy
a worship space of such divine design;
scattering the worshipers to far-off lands
where even their God will be forgotten.

Still the question preys upon my mind
as I reach the span that bridges life and death;
was it to save God's face or my own
that I spoke the easy words I hoped were true?

Or was it the arrogance of Jeremiah
standing oxen-eyed, clothed in his yoke
smug in the ugliness of his predictions,
glad in even the saddest of his prophecies.

I broke the yoke of one who burdens
the people with his sad truths.
Is it a better death to die with the misery
of all our losses dragging us downward?

Or might it just be more humane to face
our end like animals brought to slaughter
in ignorance and bliss.
I have no final answer for this.

Though I have cast my fate with blissful lies
I approach my final days bereft of comfort
finding no better companion in bright falsehood
than in the dark and terrible unraveling of truth.

I had only wanted to say a good word
to restore the light to eyes gone dull

Now as my own sight dims
I can see everything all too well.
Now I would be all too glad to sing
my song in any distant land my God appointed,
to build a house and till a field, to wait
and seek the welfare of a city filled with strangers.

(Michael E. Williams)

Although there were many prophets in the ancient world, not all of their prophesies were written down. The only ones that were put in writing were those that would be needed by later generations. (*Sefer Ha-Aggadah* 480.104)

The World Restored

The exiles long to come home and celebrate a new covenant, a dream of consolation that is written on their hearts.

The Story

At that time, says the LORD, I shall be the God of all the families of Israel, and they will be my people. These are the words of the LORD:

A people that escaped the sword
found favour in the wilderness.
The Lord went to give rest to Israel;
from afar he appeared to them:
I have dearly loved you from of old,
and still I maintain my unfailing care
  for you.
Virgin Israel, I shall build you up
  again,
and you will be rebuilt.
Again you will provide yourself with
  tambourines,
and go forth with the merry throng
  of dancers.
Again you will plant vineyards on
  the hills of Samaria,
and those who plant them will
  enjoy the fruit;
for a day will come when the
  watchmen
cry out on Ephraim's hills,
Come, let us go up to Zion,
to the LORD our God.'

For these are the words of the LORD:

Break into shouts of joy for Jacob's
  sake,
lead the nations, crying loud and
  clear,

sing out your praises and say:
'The Lord has saved his people;
he has preserved a remnant of
  Israel.'
See how I bring them from a
  northern land;
I shall gather them from the far
  ends of the earth,
among them the blind and lame,
the woman with child and the
  woman in labour.
A vast company, they come home,
weeping as they come,
but I shall comfort them and be their
  escort.
I shall lead them by streams of
  water;
their path will be smooth, they will
  not stumble.
For I have become a father to Israel,
and Ephraim is my eldest son.
Listen to the word of the LORD, you
  nations,
announce it, make it known to
  coastlands far away:
He who scattered Israel will gather
  them again
and watch over them as a shepherd
  watches his flock.
For the LORD has delivered Jacob
and redeemed him from a foe too
  strong for him.
They will come with shouts of joy to
  Zion's height,
radiant at the bounty of the LORD:

127

the grain, the new wine, and the oil,
the young of flock and herd.
They will be like a well-watered
    garden
and never languish again.
Girls will then dance for joy,
and men young and old will rejoice;
I shall turn their grief into gladness,
comfort them, and give them joy
    after sorrow.
I shall satisfy the priests with the fat
    of the land
and my people will have their fill of
    my bounty.
This is the word of the LORD.

....

The days are coming, says the
LORD, when I shall sow Israel and
Judah with the seed of man and the
seed of cattle. As I watched over them
with intent to pull down and to uproot,
to demolish and destroy and inflict
disaster, so now I shall watch over
them to build and to plant. This is the
word of the LORD.

In those days it will no longer be said,
'Parents have eaten sour grapes

and the children's teeth are set on
    edge';

for everyone will die for his own wrongdoing; he who eats the sour grapes
will find his own teeth set on edge.

The days are coming, says the
LORD, when I shall establish a new
covenant with the people of Israel and
Judah. It will not be like the covenant
I made with their forefathers when I
took them by the hand to lead them
out of Egypt, a covenant they broke,
though I was patient with them, says
the LORD. For this is the covenant I
shall establish with the Israelites after
those days, says the LORD: I shall set
my law within them, writing it on their
hearts; I shall be their God, and they
will be my people. No longer need
they teach one another, neighbour or
brother, to know the LORD; all of them,
high and low alike, will know me, says
the LORD, for I shall forgive their
wrongdoing, and their sin I shall call
to mind no more.

Comments on the Story

The reader of Jeremiah will want to linger over the multiplicity of words and images found in Jeremiah 30–31. These chapters form an entity often called the "Book of Consolation," and within them the visions of the restored people spring to life. Chapter 30:1 provides the context. Jeremiah is to write down Yahweh's words for the days would surely be coming when the fortunes of Yahweh's people, Israel and Judah, are restored.

What follows this brief introduction is not an extended narrative about the exiled peoples and how and when they would return. Rather, the two chapters consist of terse imagery, a succession of "photographic shots" that enable the reader to visualize the people who have been returned to the land given their ancestors. Woven throughout is language of the covenant—the reminder that once again Yahweh will be the God of the people, and the people will be the people of Yahweh.

While no texts from Jeremiah 30 appear in the lectionary, chapter 31 is used with great frequency. Units from this chapter are used on Easter (vv. 1-6), during Pentecost (vv. 7-9 and 27-34), on the second Sunday of Christmas (vv. 7-14), and during Lent (vv. 31-34). Perhaps this vast distribution reminds us that during every season of the year we need to be reminded of God's power to restore and renew us.

The first unit (vv. 2-6) is rich with the imagery of rejoicing. The sound of the tambourines and the sight of the dancing community bring to the reader an air of excitement and celebration at what God has wrought. Undergirding the restoration are two important theological affirmations—God loves with an everlasting love and God continues to be faithful (v. 3). The following text (vv. 7-9) describes the great homecoming—the people will be brought home and gathered in from even the farthest parts of the earth. The description of the dispersed traveling home together captures the imagination of the storyteller for there are among those making the journey the blind, the lame, those pregnant with child, and those giving birth. The people are in tears as they walk back to the home they have not seen in many years—or to a home some perhaps have never seen—but a home nonetheless that has been kept alive in their memories, in their hearts and minds, through the ever-constant recital of the stories of their ancestors past. The company is blessed with water along the way—they are not seen traveling through the wasted wilderness. Their way is made straight so that they do not stumble.

With same sentiment, but different metaphor, the following unit (vv. 10-14) depicts the one gathering the dispersed as the shepherd. Those who are returning home are like a flock of sheep. The shepherd is one who gathers, and who now ransoms and redeems the community. In response there is a great rejoicing over the bounty the people now receive. Again there is dance, there is joy. The picture is one not only of joy but also of contentment. The people are satisfied.

The final lectionary text in Jeremiah 31:31-34 uses explicit covenant language; the text describes not the joyful exuberance of a people returning to their home but their renewed beings. Yahweh "cuts" a *new covenant* (a term used nowhere else in the Old Testament) with the people of Israel. Now the law will be written upon their hearts; the covenant is at the same time restored and new. This covenant will not be broken for they will all know Yahweh. The four-fold assertions on the part of Yahweh make it clear that it is Yahweh taking the initiative in this new relationship with the people. Yahweh states:

> I will make the covenant with the house of Israel;
> I will put my law within them;
> I will write it on their hearts;
> I will be their God, and they shall be my people. (see vv. 31-33 NRSV)

This compelling picture of the God whose love is everlasting comes to completion in the last line of the text "I will forgive their iniquity, and remember their sin no more" (v. 34 NRSV).

Often unnoticed in this text regarding the new covenant is the assertion that all will know Yahweh in this new covenantal relationship—from the least to the greatest. In this new world, there will be no special revelation. Inherent in the vision is an equality and an inclusivity. From our New Testament perspective, which cannot be overlooked, this new covenant is not for a chosen few; it is for everyone. The storyteller is intrigued. What would the world be like if every creature knew Yahweh and lived life as God's preferred person?

If every creature knew Yahweh and behaved accordingly, we might not know firsthand the pain of Rachel, mother of Joseph and Benjamin (31:15-17). The poignant picture of a mother who has lost her children is used as the foil to the picture of redemption, of what could be possible. This portrait of unbearable grief is used in contrast to the wonderful hope for the future that is envisioned. Rachel weeps bitterly for her lost children; God speaks to her saying, "Keep your voice from weeping, and your eyes from tears; for there is a reward for your work, says the LORD: they shall come back from the land of the enemy; there is hope for your future, . . . your children shall come back to their own country" (31:16-17 NRSV).

The metaphor of the parent/child relationship is also invoked in verses 18-20. Yahweh acknowledges that as often as Yahweh has been called to speak against the child, still the child is remembered. Yahweh is moved by the memory of him, and Yahweh will have mercy on Ephraim. God's attachment to Rachel's child, Ephraim, is as strong as the attachment of the mother. God's love is that strong and that everlasting.

Any one of these images in Jeremiah 31 (many recalled from the stories of Israel's matriarchs and patriarchs) could be a fruitful seed for a story about the redemption and restoration of God's people—the bringing in of the fertile harvest, the great homecoming of everyone, even the one who is not yet born, the writing of the covenant on the heart, or the shepherd gathering in the fold. But perhaps more in keeping with the disjointed form of the two chapters of the Book of Consolation, the storyteller could tell short vignettes, images of hopeful future, images of a world restored when the covenant with Yahweh is maintained. As one image builds upon another, the collage grows, until there is represented in its midst the likeness of everyone upon the earth, until there is none among us who feels exiled and who cannot find home.

Retelling the Story

The old man dozed almost every sunny afternoon, and in his dreams he always returned home. Though he had not lived there since he was a youngster, whenever he thought of home it was that house and that vineyard he envisioned. He was quite sure that the foreigners who had driven his family out had likely torn the house down and allowed the vines to lay in the ground until they rotted. In his dreams, though, the house and all that surrounded it were as they had been half a century ago.

The actual circumstances of his family's leaving were not at all pleasant. The soldiers had come and accused his father of being a soldier in civilian clothes. Despite the fact that his right arm hung uselessly at his side making it impossible for him to hold a weapon the invaders proceeded to beat the father senseless. Though just a child he had tried to intervene and was struck with a club so hard that he spent much of the rest of the day unconscious. When he awoke his father was dead and his family on the way into exile. He had not seen his home since.

He often thought of his father and wondered where he was buried, though he knew that, at best, his father's corpse was likely thrown into a mass grave by the invaders. His father would have been buried not so much out of respect but to keep down the stench of rotting flesh. He prayed to the One God for his father as often as he thought of him. It was all he could do under the circumstances. The feeling of helplessness had crept down deep into his bones from the day he had failed to protect his father and the rest of the family. By now helplessness had become his constant companion.

Each day of his life was accompanied by another constant—the bitter aftertaste of exile. It never left him so that even his dreams were tinged with it. Each afternoon when he visited his childhood home he returned with that same deep sense of loss he had experienced that first day. Except now, over half a century later he would call the roll of his losses. Three brothers and two sisters gone. First a father then a mother gone. Two wives gone. Three sons gone. Two daughters gone. All gone. Not to mention aunts and uncles. Not to mention cousins. Not to mention, except in his silent daily prayers, the place of prayer, the center of the universe, the holy mountain gone. All gone.

Sometimes in the wee hours of the night, when the earth and all that is on it are covered in darkness he thought he could hear crying. In some distant house on another shadowy street someone was weeping inconsolably. Some wife grieving for her husband or some child calling for its mother. Or perhaps it was Rachel weeping for her children. At first the exiles talked of their pain and loneliness and sang the songs of their pilfered homeland. But no longer. Their yearnings went unspoken, and if they wept and tore their clothes in grief they did so under the cover of darkness.

The most terrible question was one that most of the exiles could not even bring themselves to speak. Why would God allow their land to be taken, their homes occupied by their enemies, their holy places desecrated? When they were forced to forsake their homeland, did their God forsake them as well? When their holy place of worship fell, did God abandon it? Had God abandoned them, too? These were the questions whose answers were too horrifying to consider. They lay beneath every phrase uttered by the exiles, were the very breath that carried their words along. They were the tune to each of the songs they sang,

The sages say that Rachel, their foremother, takes up for the people who are cast out as exiles. She pleads with God saying, "My father gave my sister to the man I loved, who loved me. He worked for seven years for the right to marry me. Then my sister took my place. I didn't shame my sister or cast her out. If I can accept my sister after what my father did, why cannot you accept the people after all they have done?" Then she weeps for her children, the exiles. It is only then that God relents and says that one day the exiled will return. (*Sefer Ha-Aggadah* 148.12)

and were the very substance of their dreams.

The old man had made a certain peace with the tormenting ambiguity of his situation. His daily visits home were his substitute for hope. In others, such dreams drove them to despair, even suicide. But he knew that as long as there were dreams of home there was hope. As long as there was hope there was the possibility that God had not abandoned the people or the land. The old man would cling to that hope as long as there was breath in his body and blood in his veins.

Today he finished his prayers and his midday meal. He sat in the sunshine and drank tea from a glass. He closed his eyes and could hear his own breathing. Each outward-flowing current of air was a prayer for the restoration of the people. He could count the rhythmic music of his heartbeats and it was the song of the wanderer searching for home. He listened and heard no weeping; Rachel was quiet now, the memory of her children a silent regret. He could see constellations against the night sky of his eyelids and wondered if they were the same stars his ancestor had peered at so many centuries ago when God had promised that her descendants would be a great nation. Was his people's exile just like the exile she had experienced when Ibrahim's other wife had sent her and her child away to die in the wilderness? God had not abandoned them then. Why would God abandon him now?

Once again on his dream journey home he heard the call to prayer issuing from the minaret. His lips began to form the ancient words of faith, "There is no God but Allah and Mohammed is his prophet." *(Michael E. Williams)*

The people were like the king's son who left home and took on a very self-indulgent and destructive way of life. The king sent word to his son asking him to turn back from the ways that would destroy him and return home. The boy responded through a note that said, "After all that I have done I am ashamed to stand in your presence." The father sent word again saying, "Are you not my son? Am I not your father? Don't you realize to whom you would be returning? I am your father and I will always be waiting to receive you." Just so, God waits to receive the people and welcome them on their return. (*Deuteronomy Rabbah* 2.24-25)

A Wise Investment

Jeremiah buys a field from his cousin, so he can reclaim it when the refugees return.

The Story

The word which came to Jeremiah from the Lord in the tenth year of King Zedekiah of Judah, which was the eighteenth year of Nebuchadrezzar. At that time the forces of the Babylonian king were besieging Jerusalem, and the prophet Jeremiah was imprisoned in the court of the guardhouse attached to the royal palace. King Zedekiah had imprisoned him after demanding what he meant by this prophecy: 'These are the words of the LORD: I shall give this city into the power of the king of Babylon, and he will capture it. Nor will King Zedekiah of Judah escape from the Chaldaeans; he will be surrendered to the king of Babylon and will speak with him face to face and see him with his own eyes. Zedekiah will be taken to Babylon and will remain there until the day I visit him, says the LORD. However much you fight against the Chaldaeans you will have no success.'

Jeremiah said: This word of the LORD came to me: Hanamel son of your uncle Shallum is coming to you; he will say, 'Buy my field at Anathoth; as next-of-kin you have the right of redemption to buy it.' Just as the LORD had foretold, my cousin Hanamel came to me in the court of the guardhouse and said, 'Buy my field at Anathoth in Benjamin. You have the right of redemption and possession as next-of-kin, so buy it for yourself.'

I recognized that this instruction came from the LORD, so I bought the field at Anathoth from my cousin Hanamel and weighed out the price for him, seventeen shekels of silver. I signed and sealed the deed, had it witnessed, and then weighed the money on the scales. I took my copies of the deed of purchase, both the sealed and the unsealed copies, and handed them over to Baruch son of Neriah, son of Mahseiah, in the presence of Hanamel my cousin and the witnesses whose names were subscribed on the deed of purchase, and of the Judaeans sitting in the court of the guardhouse. In their presence I gave my instructions to Baruch: These are the words of the LORD of Hosts the God of Israel: Take these copies of the deed of purchase, both the sealed and the unsealed copies, and deposit them in an earthenware jar so that they may be preserved for a long time to come. For these are the words of the LORD of Hosts the God of Israel: Houses, fields and vineyards will again be bought and sold in this land.

Comments on the Story

The story takes place in the tenth year of King Zedekiah of Judah. The king of Babylon is besieging Jerusalem, and Jeremiah is imprisoned in the palace of the Judean king. As readers of Jeremiah we would expect that Jeremiah has been imprisoned for speaking harsh and difficult words to the king. We are right. The editor relates to the reader the words Jeremiah has spoken; the words speak of the demise of the community and of the king who will be taken into exile. As readers we wonder why this narrative account of Jeremiah in prison is placed here between the oracles of restoration in chapters 30, 31, and 33. Why is this story about a land transaction placed here when chronologically, it would be more appropriately placed later in the extended narrative? We must read the story to find out.

Abruptly the attention of the reader changes. The words of Zedekiah trail off and suddenly our attention is focused on the words of Jeremiah, who recounts a word he has received from Yahweh. Jeremiah is told that his cousin Hanamel will come to him in prison and offer to him the right to purchase a piece of property at Anathoth. When his cousin appears and makes the offer, Jeremiah is certain that Yahweh has spoken.

Time slows as the narrator recounts for the reader the intricate details of the business agreement made between Jeremiah and his cousin. Jeremiah weighs out the money, seventeen shekels of silver, signs the deed, seals it, gets witnesses and weighs the money on scales. He takes the sealed deed of purchase that contains the terms of the agreement, and gives the deed to Baruch in the presence of his cousin. Jeremiah speaks: "Thus says the LORD of hosts, the God of Israel. Take these deeds, both this sealed deed of purchase and this open deed, and put them in an earthenware jar, in order that they may last for a long time. For thus says the LORD of hosts, the God of Israel: Houses and fields and vineyards shall again be bought in this land" (vv. 14-15 NRSV). As the transfer of the property is witnessed, Jeremiah himself recounts for the witnesses the theological import of the transaction being made. As if answering their unspoken questions about the wisdom of investing in land, which at that very moment is being besieged and destroyed by a large foreign power, Jeremiah espouses a word of hope. Some day, Jeremiah says, there will again be fields and houses and vineyards in the land (v. 15).

As the theological statement is rendered, the reader becomes aware of the importance of this narrative set so carefully between chapters 31 and 33. In the buying of the property at a time when the community despairs, Jeremiah renders visible the hope that the oracles in the Book of Consolation espouse, the hope that some day, once again, the people will be able to live on the land.

The dialogue continues, that is, the conversation between Jeremiah and God continues in the form of a prayer. It is unusual to find a prayer in the Jeremianic text; its presence and importance is heightened for the reader. We want to hear what Jeremiah says to Yahweh. Is he confident about the purchase he has made? Does he really hold fast to the hope that while now all seems to be lost, in the future something might be gained? Can one put trust in Yahweh when every visible, tangible sign would lead one to abandon all hope? Verses 16-44 tell the rest of the story. They are filled with flashbacks and projections into the future.

The prayer of Jeremiah is a human prayer. It is our prayer. It is a prayer of praise and affirmation to the God who has created the heavens and the earth and who has wrought great deeds of deliverance for God's people. The prayer is one of confession; Jeremiah acknowledges the sin of the community that, throughout history, has not heard the voice of Yahweh. And ultimately, Jeremiah's prayer is one that expresses disbelief. "See, the siege ramps have been cast up against the city to take it, and the city, faced with sword, famine, and pestilence, has been given into the hands of the Chaldeans who are fighting against it. What you spoke has happened, as you yourself can see. Yet you, O LORD GOD, have said to me, 'Buy the field for money and get witnesses'—though the city has been given into the hands of the Chaldeans" (vv. 24-25 NRSV).

Jeremiah has been delivering the oracles of hope and salvation from Yahweh to Yahweh's people. But in the act of buying his cousin's property, Jeremiah was asked to invest in that future—stake what was his on that future. Don't you see, Jeremiah said to Yahweh, that the siege-ramps are set in place and the city is faced with destruction? How hard it was for Jeremiah to believe what he himself professed to Yahweh—"Nothing is too hard for you."

Jeremiah's profession is echoed in Yahweh's own words (vv. 26-44), "I am the LORD, the God of all flesh; is anything too hard for me" (v. 26 NRSV)? The answer to the rhetorical question is, of course, no. In great detail Yahweh recounts the history of the relationship between Yahweh and the people. In great detail Yahweh recounts the future that will come to that same people. Though disaster is upon them, Yahweh assures them that restoration will come, when once again people will buy fields and homes in the land that will be returned to them (v. 44).

There is no response from Jeremiah who remains imprisoned in the king's palace. But he must wonder if has made a wise investment. Or perhaps the investment he has made fortifies and strengthens him. He sits in his confinement wondering if what he has been called to proclaim is really true—no disaster can take away a hope that is grounded in God.

Retelling the Story

Excerpt from the journal of Baruch, a scribe:

It has been quite a ride, this time I have spent taking down the words of the prophet. It has taken me places I never expected to go. Today I went to prison to visit him. I have no idea if I will be able to return there again. Nebuchadrezzar and the Babylonian army are at the city gate. In fact that is the reason for Jeremiah's imprisonment. He told the king, "These are the words of the Lord: I shall give this city into the power of the king of Babylon, and he will capture it." Zedekiah asked the prophet what he meant by these words. It seemed to me perfectly apparent that God meant to give Jerusalem over into the hands of Nebuchadrezzar. Perhaps it was the king's desire to hear words of success rather than words of defeat and capture that drove him to ask for another interpretation. I have always thought that my employer was too honest for his own good, but then again, I am no prophet.

Today, however, when I arrived at the prison there was no message of doom for Zedekiah. Rather, Jeremiah had his mind on real estate. He said to me, "Baruch, my friend, we are going to buy some land." This news startled me a bit. Though I am not a man practiced in things of the world, I do know enough to avoid buying property that is about to be conquered by an enemy army. "Do you think that's wise?" was all I could bring myself to ask.

"Wise, my child, of course it is wise. It is God's bidding." I realized at that point of the conversation that there was no use in my talking practicality to the prophet. Once he became convinced that it was what God wanted of him there was no talking sense to him. Behavior that other, more rational people, would have dismissed out of hand Jeremiah embraced if the voice of God had announced it to him. That is what makes him so interesting—and so dangerous.

So I sat down to write. But this time there were no grand visions to record. Instead, the prophet asked me to write out a deed and a contract for the exchange of property. This was the sort of work I had done in the

> When Jeremiah affirms that God is the creator of heaven and earth, it means more than first appears. According to the sages, it means that before a thought is thought or a word spoken, God knows it. Even before each creature appeared on the earth God knew its nature. Clearly, the Creator of all knows the creation intimately. (*Genesis Rabbah* 9.3)

136

years before I met him. I always thought of it as ordinary work. But this was no ordinary task since we were living in no ordinary time. Besides it was not my decision. From what he said to me it was not even Jeremiah's decision. He told me his cousin Hanamel had come to him in the court of the guardhouse and offered to sell him property in Anathoth, since he was the nearest kinsman and had the right to redeem the land. How you can redeem land that is about to fall into the hands of your enemy is beyond me. The prophet in his typically enigmatic fashion told me that it really didn't matter if I could fathom such business transactions, that only God could redeem the land in any case.

So the property was purchased for seventeen shekels of silver. The deed was signed and sealed. The silver was weighed and given to Hanamel. As the sound of Babylonian armies carried over the city wall a piece of land was sold; a piece of land was bought, land that in a few days would be worthless. Common wisdom dictates that prophets who prophesy doom do not invest in real estate. There was something I had learned by hard experience: Jeremiah was no common prophet nor did he serve a common God.

Many in this world seem to think that they can manage, even control, their God. The Babylonians I hear can bribe and cajole their deities into conveying upon them health, wealth, and even fertility, or so they believe. If they are victorious they will offer thanks to one of their gods but really will be ascribing power to an incantation of their own concoction and a stone image of their own making.

I have learned that idolatry is simply self-worship once removed. We say a prayer and the gods are coerced by our words into answering it to our satisfaction. We make an offering of food, and well-fed deities return the favor. We carve a reflection of our own face and worship it as our God. We lay with prostitutes to sate our lust and imagine thereby to fertilize our fields. Even we who worship the one true God can succumb to the easy lies of idolatry. Without those God-crazed Jeremiahs among us we would fall more often.

The prophet is at his prayers and I am recording this outlandish transaction. Perhaps in times like these our only hope is found in such outrageous faith. There are those who will lay their lives and goods on the line for a future only God can know. These are the Jeremiahs of the world. Others of us can only stand aside and marvel at such faith or foolishness. And we can record for future generations the lives and words of God's outrageous faithful. We are the Baruchs. We each have our role. God help us all. (Michael E. Williams)

The Shock of Reconciliation

Hosea and Gomer marry and have children, but . . .

The Story

THE word of the LORD which came to Hosea son of Beeri during the reigns of Uzziah, Jotham, Ahaz, and Hezekiah, kings of Judah, and during the reign of Jeroboam son of Joash king of Israel.

THIS is the beginning of the LORD'S message given by Hosea. He said, 'Go and take an unchaste woman as your wife, and with this woman have children; for like an unchaste woman this land is guilty of unfaithfulness to the LORD.' So he married Gomer daughter of Diblaim, and she conceived and bore him a son. The LORD said to Hosea, 'Call him Jezreel, for in a little while I am going to punish the dynasty of Jehu for the blood shed in the valley of Jezreel, and bring the kingdom of Israel to an end. On that day I shall break Israel's bow in the vale of Jezreel.' Gomer conceived again and bore a daughter, and the LORD said to Hosea,

Call her Lo-ruhamah;
for I shall never again show love to Israel,
never again forgive them.

But Judah I shall love and save.
I shall save them not by bow or sword or weapon of war,
not by horses and horsemen,
but I shall save them by the LORD their God.

After weaning Lo-ruhamah, Gomer conceived and bore a son; and the LORD said,

Call him Lo-ammi;
for you are not my people,
and I shall not be your God.
The Israelites will be as countless as the sands of the sea,
which can neither be measured nor numbered;
it will no longer be said to them,
'You are not my people';
they will be called Children of the Living God.
The people of Judah and of Israel will be reunited
and will choose for themselves one leader;
they will spring up from the land,
for great will be the day of Jezreel.
You are to say to your brothers,
'You are my people,'
and to your sisters, 'You are loved.'

Call your mother to account,
for she is no longer my wife
nor am I her husband.
Let her put an end to her infidelity
and banish the lovers from her bosom,
or else I shall strip her bare
and parade her naked as the day she was born.
I shall make her bare as the wilderness,

138

parched as the desert,
and leave her to die of thirst.
I shall show no love towards her
children,
for they are the offspring of adultery.
Their mother has been promiscuous;
she who conceived them is
shameless.
She says, 'I will go after my lovers,
who supply me with food and drink,
with my wool and flax, my oil and
perfumes.'
That is why I shall close her road
with thorn bushes
and obstruct her path with a wall,
so that she can no longer find a way
through.
Though she pursues her lovers
she will not overtake them,
though she looks for them
she will not find them.
At last she will say,
'I shall go back to my husband
again,
for I was better off then than I am
now.'
She does not know that it was I who
gave her
the grain, the new wine, and fresh
oil,
I who lavished on her silver and gold
which they used for the Baal.

That is why I am going to take back
my grain at the harvest and my new
wine at the vintage,
take away the wool and the flax
which I provided to cover her naked
body.
Now I shall reveal her shame to her
lovers,
and no one will rescue her from me.
I shall put a stop to all her
merrymaking,
her pilgrimages, new moons, and
sabbaths,
all her festivals.
I shall ravage the vines and the fig
trees,

of which she says, 'These are the fees
which my lovers have paid me,'
and I shall leave them to grow wild
so that beasts may eat them.
I shall punish her for the holy days
when she burnt sacrifices to the
baalim,
when she decked herself with her
rings and necklaces,
when, forgetful of me, she ran after
her lovers.
This is the word of the LORD.

But now I shall woo her,
lead her into the wilderness,
and speak words of encouragement
to her.
There I shall restore her vineyards to
her,
turning the valley of Achor into a
gate of hope;
there she will respond as in her
youth,
as when she came up from Egypt.
On that day she will call me 'My
husband'
and will no more call me 'My Baal';
I shall banish from her lips the very
names of the baalim;
never again will their names be
invoked.
This is the word of the LORD.

Then I shall make a covenant on
Israel's behalf with the wild beasts,
the birds of the air, and the creatures that creep on the ground, and
I shall break bow and sword and
weapon of war and sweep them off
the earth, so that my people may
lie down without fear. I shall
betroth you to myself for ever,
bestowing righteousness and justice, loyalty and love; I shall betroth
you to myself, making you faithful,
and you will know the LORD. At that
time I shall answer, says the LORD;
I shall answer the heavens and they

139

will answer the earth, and the earth
will answer the grain, the new wine,
and fresh oil, and they will answer
Jezreel. Israel will be my new sow-
ing in the land, and I shall show
love to Lo-ruhamah and say to Lo-
ammi, 'You are my people, and he
will say, 'You are my God.'

. . . .

ISRAEL, hear the word of the LORD;
for the LORD has a charge to bring
against the inhabitants of the land:
There is no good faith or loyalty,

no acknowledgement of God in the
land.
People swear oaths and break them;
they kill and rob and commit
adultery;
there is violence, one deed of blood
after another.
Therefore the land will be desolate
and all who live in it will languish,
with the wild beasts and the birds of
the air;
even the fish will vanish from the
sea.

Comments on the Story

The story of Hosea and Gomer found in Hosea 1–3 serves as the prelude to the oracles from Yahweh delivered to the Northern Kingdom of Israel found in chapters 4–14. It thus serves to provide the trajectory through which the remaining chapters are read; its purpose is to provide for the reader an understanding of the relationship between Yahweh and Israel as embodied through the relationship of prophet and wife.

It is Yahweh who first speaks. The word from Yahweh comes to Hosea thus, "Go, take for yourself a wife of whoredom and have children of whoredom, for the land commits great whoredom by forsaking the LORD" (v. 2 NRSV). It is clear from these first words that the message from Yahweh is coming in response to the people's lack of faithfulness. They are as a "wife of whoredom"—that is, perpetually promiscuous and unfaithful. They have forsaken.

Time becomes compressed; in six short verses we find that Hosea is obedient to the initial word from Yahweh. He takes a wife named Gomer, and together they bring forth three children. Yahweh intervenes at the birth of the children to offer their appropriate names—Jezreel, Lo-ruhamah (not pitied) and Lo-ammi (not my people). The names are significant; they graphically depict the plight of the people and the seriousness of their offenses. Yahweh will extend no more pity to them; perhaps even the covenant tie will be broken and God will no longer be the god of the people.

This is a shocking story! We have heard it so often, however, that the images no longer haunt us. What would it be like if God no longer had pity? What would it be like to no longer be God's people? We are no longer shocked by these words, and the questions elude us.

In chapter 2 the reader gets a glimpse of the desperation of a spouse whose partner has been unfaithful. It is to the children that Yahweh speaks: "Plead with your mother, plead—for she is not my wife, and I am not her husband"

(v. 1 NRSV). That which was feared has come to pass. The relationship between partners is broken, and as if in a court of law, the indictment is read. The woman has been adulterous, but she is offered an alternative. She is to put away her "whoring" and her adultery or she will be stripped, made like a wasteland; she will die of thirst (v. 3). The woman has been deceived. She thinks that all the wonderful things of life—the bread, water, wool, flax, oil, and drink (v. 5)—have come not from Yahweh, but from her lovers.

The three-fold consequences for the woman's unfaithfulness are recounted in verses 6, 9, and 14. (Note the introductory word "therefore" in each of these verses in the NRSV.) In the initial unit (vv. 6-8) Yahweh's first response is described. Yahweh's first inclination is to lock the spouse in and make it impossible for her to find her lovers. Only then would the woman know that it was her spouse, Yahweh, who had given her the gifts of grain, wine, oil, gold, and silver. The second unit (vv. 9-13) describes intensified feelings of Yahweh toward the spouse. The rush of rhetoric betrays anger that is aggressively and destructively displayed. Seven consecutive verbs describe what Yahweh will do to the spouse. The woman is now not simply confined; she is humiliated. Joy is taken from her. Those things that she thought she had received from her lovers are all destroyed. She is punished.

The reader expects, then, in the third unit for the anger and hostility of the forsaken spouse to reach even more intense proportion. We expect perhaps even death will be the consequence of the unfaithfulness of this woman. We are surprised at the words that follow, "Therefore, I will now allure her, and bring her into the wilderness, and speak tenderly to her" (v. 14 NRSV). This is shocking reconciliation! When we least expect it, the final word is for restoration and grace. Yahweh conceives of the day that the relationship with Yahweh's people will be as it had been in the early days when the relationship was new, when the people were led out of Egypt. In the climactic moment, we witness God's nostalgia for the way things were. It will not be difficult for the contemporary storyteller to think of similar circumstances where differences seem to be irreconcilable. It is harder for us to imagine that irreconcilable differences are, in the end, reconcilable. The message of Hosea is that with God it is possible.

The covenant that is restored (2:16-20) is one that affects all of the earth and its creatures—the wild animals, birds, and creeping things. The people of Israel will then be safe, and there will be war no more. The new covenant is one that will last forever, and the vows incorporate the most important and cherished concepts of the Israelite cult. Yahweh will take the people in *righteousness, in justice, in steadfast love and in mercy.* There could be no firmer foundation for a covenantal relationship between God and people. The reciting of the commitments that will be made to each other closes with a reversal of the introductory forecasts of doom. Jezreel (God sows) will once again be sown and will thrive in the land. Yahweh will have pity on "No More Pity." Yahweh will say to "Not My People" now you are my people. The people will once again claim Yahweh.

Chapter 3 forcefully returns us to the initial narrative. Though Hosea and Gomer are unnamed, Yahweh again speaks to the prophet and says, "Go, love a woman who has a lover and is an adulteress, just as the LORD loves the people of Israel, though they turn to other gods and love raisin cakes" (v. 1 NRSV). This is perhaps more shocking than the restoration described in chapter 2! Yahweh calls the prophet to again make himself vulnerable to the unfaithfulness of a spouse. We are invited to believe that in the same way, Yahweh chooses to be in relationship with Yahweh's people. To be in relationship is to make oneself susceptible to disappointment and loss.

The story of Hosea and Gomer provides the prelude for the introduction to chapter 4 that follows. An indictment is read: there is no faithfulness or loyalty, no knowledge of God in the land. How does the world act out its faithlessness? According to Hosea 4 through swearing, lying, murder, stealing, adultery, and bloodshed. We are reminded again that when the people of God are unfaithful, the consequences are global—the land and everything that lives and breathes suffers.

We read these verses in chapter 4 through the perspective found in the story of Hosea and Gomer. There we had found that though the sin and the unfaithfulness of the people was of

In reading and analyzing Hosea 1–3 we become aware of the dangers of metaphoric language. The story of Hosea and Gomer grew out of a culture where marriage customs and role definitions favored the male, who owned women and children as property. The sexual behavior of women was carefully guarded, and therefore a woman like Gomer being promiscuous was shameful. When the story of Hosea and Gomer is the metaphor through which we come to understand the relationship between Yahweh and Israel, we are in danger of making normative for ourselves the cultural expectations out of which the story grew. The reader might interpret the text to mean that men are like God, that women are sinful and unclean, that unfaithful women deserve abuse, that to be abusive is godlike, that seducing the abused spouse back into relationship is a demonstration of the love of God, or that every relationship must continue regardless of the way one human being treats another.

On the other hand, in an attempt to compensate for cultural biases, the reader might conclude that Hosea is an abusive spouse, who drove his wife from the family.

These kind of interpretations should be stripped of "normative" power. We remember here that the story is descriptive—to illustrate the love of God, who would call the unfaithful Israel back into relationship again and again and again.

immense proportion, there was the possibility of reconciliation. And so we wonder as we continue reading the book of Hosea . . . will we find there another shocking word? Another shocking word of reconciliation?

We hope so.

Retelling the Story

I couldn't believe it. Mom and Dad split up. Mom was gone. I should have known. I'd seen it happen in other homes, but ours? How could God let it happen? Throughout my childhood I heard whispers. Some children were told by their parents not to play with me. I thought maybe it was because I was Jewish and they were "uppity" Christians. I understood that not all Christians were like that, but a few seemed to think themselves better than we were. But there seemed to be more to it than this—a lot more.

Early in middle school, some boys, streetwise beyond their years, began calling one another by their mother's names. I thought it silly. But I was most uncomfortable with the way they used *my* mother's name. This little game was designed to make us younger boys flinch, but when they looked at me and said "Gomer," they tittered and turned to one another whispering. They whispered just loud enough for me to hear—yet not loud enough for me to comprehend. I knew they really were talking about her. Little snatches of conversation drifted by: "Mmm, did you ever watch the way she walks?" " . . . her clothing is . . . " "last night I saw her with . . . " On it went.

They made up little poems: "Israel, Israel, your mother's out with a fishing reel," and another would pipe up, "yes, yes, Gomer's been out fishing for men." I wanted to cry, but I would not, not then, not in front of them.

There were tensions in the home, too. Sometimes Dad would ask Mom, "What've you been doing today?" Sounded like the kind of question that either he or she might ask me or my sister. But it would send Mom off into orbit.

"Why do you want to know? What business is it of yours? Checking up on me again?" Dad would redden and get all quiet. I just wanted to yell, "Chill!" But then again, it was obviously quite cool in there already.

> When God makes all things new in the time to come, there will be ten things that God will do. The seventh of those ten will be to bring together all living creatures along with the people of Israel and make a covenant with them. This is what Hosea is speaking of when he says "Then I shall make covenant on Israel's behalf with the wild beasts, and the birds of the air, and the creatures that creep on the ground, and I shall break bow and sword and weapon of war and sweep them off the earth, so that my people may lie down without fear." (*Exodus Rabbah* 15.21)

Shortly before my younger brother was born, I overheard them fighting. Dad was saying, "That's not my child! That's not my child!" When the baby came home from the hospital, Mom didn't. Dad gave him a Hebrew name, Lo-ammi, a biblical name Dad said. His child or not, Dad cared for him like his own.

In the synagogue Dad performed his rabbinical duties as always, but there was a sadness in him. Most of the congregation understood. I didn't, but in time he told me. He told me how Yahweh called him to be a rabbi. He also told me that he loved a young lady, my mom, that people warned him would not make a good wife for a rabbi. She was a bit wild, they said. But he was drawn to her like a moth to a flame, and was even convinced that she was God's gift to him.

A king once became very angry with his wife and proclaimed that he was going to divorce her and disown their children. He said to her, "You are not my wife." Afterward when he had time for his anger to cool and he thought of the times he and his wife had shared, he decided to have a piece of jewelry made to express his newly remembered appreciation for her. When others saw the king ordering the piece of jewelry they went and told the kingdom, "The king is over his anger with the queen. We saw him having a piece of jewelry made for her. His anger is not for a season, but his care for her is forever." Just so, the sages say, God's anger is for a season only, but God's compassion is forever. (*Numbers Rabbah* 2.15)

I must say, young as I was, I thought he was looney. It was no secret that she was living with the owner of a bawdy nightclub—that she was even one of his dancing girls. I always wondered why she found that kind of life exciting. What was wrong with her family? Weren't we good enough? What had we done—worst of all, what had I done—to make life at home so unattractive? At times, Dad astounded me. "Talk to her," he'd say. "Tell your brother and sister to talk to her. Tell her to come home."

How could he think that way? She had been unfaithful—not just unfaithful, but flagrantly unfaithful—and made him and her children the laughingstock of the town.

How could he want her back? He'd tell me Bible stories about how the Almighty loved us. God's people, the beloved of our Maker, had also been repeatedly unfaithful. He used to say that all of us, in a way, have been unfaithful to our trust. He just wanted her back. "You children plead with her," he'd say. "Tell her to come home." I'd bitterly point out that she'd destroyed our family. He would say compassionately, "Yes, worse yet, she's destroying herself. I will pursue her even as our God pursues me."

Together again? Us? Some part of me even wants that to be true. We'll see how it goes. *(Ed Thorn)*

What I Desire

A great political crisis is emerging, and the Lord is choosing sides,
which is unfortunate for Israel.

The Story

Blow the trumpet in Gibeah,
the horn in Ramah,
raise the battle cry in Bethaven:
'We are with you, Benjamin!'
On the day of punishment
Ephraim will be laid waste.
This is the certain doom
I have decreed for Israel's tribes.
Judah's rulers act like men
who move their neighbour's
    boundary;
on them I shall pour out
my wrath like a flood.
Ephraim is an oppressor trampling on
    justice,
obstinately pursuing what is
    worthless.
But I am going to be a festering sore
    to Ephraim,
a canker to the house of Judah.

When Ephraim found that he was
    sick,
and Judah found that he was covered
    with sores,
Ephraim turned to Assyria
and sent envoys to the Great King.
But he had no power to cure you
or heal your sores.
I shall be fierce as a panther to
    Ephraim,
fierce as a lion to Judah;

I shall maul the prey and go,
carry it off beyond hope of rescue.
I shall return to my dwelling-place,
until in remorse they seek me
and search diligently for me in their
    distress.

Come, let us return to the LORD.
He has torn us, but he will heal us,
he has wounded us, but he will bind
    up our wounds;
after two days he will revive us,
on the third day he will raise us
to live in his presence.
Let us strive to know the LORD,
whose coming is as sure as the
    sunrise.
He will come to us like the rain,
like spring rains that water the earth.

How shall I deal with you, Ephraim?
How shall I deal with you, Judah?
Your loyalty to me is like the
    morning mist,
like dew that vanishes early.
That is why I have cut them to
    pieces by the prophets
and slaughtered them with my words:
my judgement goes forth like light.
For I require loyalty, not sacrifice,
acknowledgement of God rather than
    whole-offerings.

Comments on the Story

Hosea is the master of metaphor and simile. Throughout the fourteen short chapters of the book the reader is confronted with a multitude of images that try to capture at least part of the essence of God. The book begins with the extended metaphor, a parable, of Hosea and Gomer who, in their relationship with each other, act out the dynamics of a God who wrestles with an unfaithful people. Their narrative paves the way for a series of judgment and restoration oracles that pictures this God in surprising and often intriguing ways. God is like a bird catcher (7:12), a lion, a leopard lurking, a bear robbed of her cubs (13:7-8) and like the dew (14:5). Equally provocative are the metaphors and similes used to describe God's people Israel. They are like a cake not turned (7:8), a dove silly and without sense (7:11), a defective bow (7:16), grapes in the wilderness (9:10), a luxuriant vine (10:1), a trained heifer (10:11), morning mist, dew that goes away early, the chaff that swirls, and smoke from the window (13:3).

Metaphors and similes play a crucial role in Hosea 5:8–6:6. This text stands at the beginning of a unit (5:8–7:16) addressed to Israel at a time of political crisis. The historical limits of this particular text are admittedly difficult to define; textual and literary difficulties compound the problem. Chapters 5:8–6:6 incorporate an announcement of judgment (5:8-15), a subsequent call to confession (6:1-3), and a final responding word from Yahweh (6:4-6).

The text begins with the sounds of horns and trumpets. We as readers wonder if the news announced will be good or bad. We are disappointed, but as a reader of Hosea, we are not surprised. The announcement is again an announcement of judgment against the people of Israel. The nations have put their trust in someone or something that cannot cure or heal them (v. 13). In the first unit (5:8-15), Yahweh in first person uses striking similes to describe who Yahweh is in relation to the people—"I am like maggots to Ephraim, and like rottenness to the house of Judah" (v. 12 NRSV; consult a variety of translations for an array of suggestive translations for this verse). Additionally, "For I will be like a lion to Ephraim, and like a young lion to the house of Judah. I myself will tear and go away; I will carry off, and no one shall rescue" (v. 14 NRSV). With these images—the first describing a gradual wearing away of the nations, and the second describing a more sudden and vicious destruction—Yahweh through the prophet, announces the fate of the people. It is then that Yahweh will return and wait until the people acknowledge their guilt and seek Yahweh's face. With that distressing thought the unit seems to come to closure. The people are carried away; Yahweh waits to see if they will return in their distress to beg for favor (5:15).

Juxtaposed to this picture of the waiting Yahweh is an observation that highlights the response of the people, "Come, let us return to the LORD . . . " (6:1).

The reader is not kept in suspense. Yahweh's ploy has worked. The people acknowledge that their plight has been brought upon them by Yahweh. Yet they believe that the one who has torn (see v. 14) will heal them. The firm conviction of the worshipers is most surprising to the reader. In their present circumstance of being torn and struck down, they affirm the restorative power of a God who will surely revive them and raise them up (v. 2). The metaphors that the people use to describe this God stand in sharp contrast to the brutal language that God has used to describe divine attributes. God's appearing is to the people like the surety of dawn. God is like the spring rains that water the earth (v. 3). The metaphors of the people depict the healing, restorative nature of God. Their confidence brings a two-fold rhetorical question from God "What shall I do with you" (v. 4 NRSV)? This heartfelt question shows the ambiguity and frustration of a God who again turns to simile to describe God's own experience with the people. "Your love is like a morning cloud, like the dew that goes away early." The love of the people is fleeting—it burns and melts away.

Yahweh must be clear with the people—again. Many times with great clarity God has made known to the people what is really important if they are to continue to be in relationship—*steadfast love and knowledge* (v. 6). The storyteller is invited to bring to the mind of the hearers the many ways that we can deceive ourselves into thinking that what God really wants is our offerings—something far more easy to bring.

It is important for the storyteller to examine the metaphors from Hosea—the metaphors that were used for a certain place and at a certain time to describe a people's experience of God. Do we know God as a prowling lion, or as rottenness? Do we know God to be sure as the dawn or as nourishing and refreshing as the spring rain? We are called upon to choose metaphors that describe who God is and has been in our lives.

Do we see our own lives and the lives of our communities reflected in the words of Yahweh to the Israelite community? Do we know that our own love for God is like a morning cloud that goes away early? Yes, surely and sadly we do. Perhaps we, like the worshiping community of Hosea's time, can say, "Come, let us return to the LORD. . . . " Then we, too, will be healed.

Retelling the Story

The Lion was king of Beulah Land. No one doubted that. When he roared, the very ground shuddered, like newly molded Jell-O during a California earthquake. It was foolhardy to disregard him. Not only was he the king, he was the creator of this universe. He created the rocks, the trees, the grass, the animals. He knew everything inside out. He knew the forces that kept the things running. He knew his subjects like they were a part of himself, indeed some said that in one sense they were. Because he understood all this so well, the lion also knew what worked well, and what didn't. He knew how to fix things when some of his obstreperous subjects did disorderly things that caused injury and chaos. Though he held the ultimate power in this universe, and could have imposed his control, the Lion wanted his subjects to choose for themselves whether to depend on and follow him. Sometimes they did not choose to obey him. It made him sad, not out of self-pity but because he recognized they could be hurt by the results of their choices.

> God often answers prayer in ways that are unexpected, the rabbis taught. As children ask for things that are unsuitable for them, so we often pray for things that will not serve our true welfare. Instead of giving us what we asked for, God gives us what we really need. For example, the children of Israel would ask for rain, which is a good thing in times of drought but destructive in flood times. What God gave Israel is the dew, which is desirable every day. (*Sefer Ha-Aggadah* 347.107)

One day the sheep that lived in the land of Ish began to quibble and quarrel with one another. But instead of seeking out the Great Lion for wisdom and advice, they went to war with one another. The long-tailed sheep of the North didn't like the ruler-ram who was a broad-tailed sheep from the South. They said he taxed too much. They didn't quite agree either on the way to worship the Great Lion. Some, indeed, worshiped other animals besides the Lion. The Southern broad-tailed sheep, however, were loyal to the Lion. As a result of the war, the sheep became separate nations. Ish was still the name of the Northern Kingdom. Jud was the name of the Southern Kingdom.

Each nation was now weaker than when both were united. Other nations saw opportunity to invade. Ish and Jud each got scared. Did they seek the Great Lion to help them? No! Some from both kingdoms said, "Let us form an alliance with great elephants to the south in the kingdom of Gyp." Others said, "No. Let us seek the assistance of the wild asses to the north in the kingdom of Syr. The wild asses were glad to help, but they subjugated and taxed the sheep heavily for those services.

The Great Lion shook his head with alarm and dismay. "Jud ought not to be changing the boundary markers that divide their property," he roared. "But, Ish has no one to blame but itself for its weakness. I will be like rotten wood to Ish. I will burst forth with my claws and rip both nations apart. I will carry them off. No one will be able to rescue them, not elephants or wild asses. When they admit their foolishness, I will let them return to their land. First they must know that I have greater wisdom than they and any ally. I have greater strength than all the other animals. When they come to me, they will know how foolish they were to trust in the wild asses of Syr. And in their misery, they will come!"

Sure enough, the sheep all said, "Let us return to our Lord the Lion who has disciplined us. He is the great healer and he will fix our wounds. We have been dreadfully wrong."

It was good. Oh, it was very good to be at home with the Lion. Unfortunately the sheep, both the long tails and the broad tails, had much to learn. The broad-tailed sheep weren't welcome at the family reunions of the long tails. And the broad-tailed sheep thought they were better than the long tails. They didn't like the way the long tails worshiped the Great Lion.

> We should not rush away from our place of worship, as if we were eager to get away from our conversation with the Holy One. But it is allowed to rush to our place of worship, desiring to return to the presence of the Holy One as soon as possible. (*Sefer Ha-Aggadah* 531.236)

Actually, though the Great Lion was glad to have them back, he was still sad. The sheep did well to worship him. They offered great sacrifices and offerings to him. Their festivals were magnificent productions. But when they left their places of worship, they didn't have the character of the Great Lion. Their lives didn't acknowledge him. They not only were haughty to their cousins of the other kingdom, but they were cruel to their own brothers. And the Great Lion was known to hang his head, to say regretfully, "What shall I do with you long-tailed sheep of the North? What shall I do with you broad-tailed sheep of the South? Your love for me lasts about as long as the dew on the morning grass. Like a fog, it comes and goes quickly."

In both Ish and Jud, the sheep acted selfishly, hurtfully, and with little regard for one another. And the Great Lion was heard to roar like the crack of thunder at the axis of a lightning bolt, "This is why my judgment has gone out upon you. What I desire from you is steadfast love, not silly, shallow sacrifices. Come know me and my ways, instead of giving me burnt offerings. All the sacrifices and offerings in the world cannot help you if you do not treat your brothers with justice. How much pain will you inflict on each other and yourselves before you come to me?" *(Ed Thorn)*

> When one of the sages saw the Temple in ruins, he grieved. "The place where Israel was offered atonement is gone!" But another sage reminded the first that God had provided another means of atonement— acts of compassion and loving-kindness. Had not the prophet Hosea spoken God's words, "It is not sacrifice I wish, but deeds of loving-kindness"? (*Sefer Ha-Aggadah* 677.346)

Welcoming the Prodigal

A mother shows compassion for an adopted child who was called out of Egypt.

The Story

When Israel was a youth, I loved him;
out of Egypt I called my son;
but the more I called, the farther they went from me;
they must needs sacrifice to the baalim
and burn offerings to images.
It was I who taught Ephraim to walk,
I who took them in my arms;
but they did not know that I secured them with reins
and led them with bonds of love,
that I lifted them like a little child to my cheek,
that I bent down to feed them.
Back they will go to Egypt,
the Assyrian will be their king;
for they have refused to return to me.
The sword will be brandished in their cities
and it will make an end of their priests
and devour them because of their scheming.

My people are bent on rebellion,
but though they call in unison to Baal
he will not lift them up.

How can I hand you over, Ephraim,
how can I surrender you, Israel?
How can I make you like Admah
or treat you as Zeboyim?
A change of heart moves me,
tenderness kindles within me.
I am not going to let loose my fury,
I shall not turn and destroy Ephraim,
for I am God, not a mortal;
I am the Holy One in your midst.
I shall not come with threats.

They will follow the LORD
who roars like a lion, and when he roars,
his sons will speed out of the west.
They will come speedily like birds out of Egypt,
like pigeons from Assyria,
and I shall settle them in their own homes.
This is the word of the LORD.

Comments on the Story

In Hosea 1–3 the husband/wife metaphor is used to bring a compelling picture of the relationship between Yahweh and the community of God's people. After a series of oracles that brings words of accusation and threat to this same community (chapters 4–10) the reader of Hosea encounters another metaphor,

150

one equally compelling. Here Yahweh is as a parent, perhaps a mother, who is mourning the impending loss of her adopted child.

The story in Hosea 11:1-11 is every bit as powerful and perhaps more poignant than the well-known parable of the "prodigal" son (Luke 15:11-32). In the Lucan parable the narrative begins as the father of two sons receives a request from the younger child who wants his portion of the family inheritance. The request is granted. The child leaves and in a distant country squanders all that he has in a famine-ridden land. Remembering the comforts of home, he returns with the intention of asking that he be treated like a hired hand. But the father, seeing him on the road is filled with compassion and runs to embrace and kiss his son. The celebration begins.

In Hosea 11 we also meet in provocative metaphor the story of a parent and child. Again the child moves away from the parent (v. 2). As readers, however, we feel even more intensely the grief of this suffering parent who stops and recalls the tender moments of the child's early years, the moments when the bonds between parent and child were young, yet strong. I remember, Yahweh says, when I taught the child to take his first steps (v. 3). I remember when I reached out and took the child up in my arms to comfort and heal him (v. 3). I led my child with compassion; we were bound in love (v. 4). I remember lifting my child to feel the softness of his cheek. I bent down to give him food (v. 4).

Like a photo album that catches all the wonderful moments of family life as a child is learning and growing, Yahweh recounts the intimate moments Yahweh has shared with Yahweh's people. The poignant rendering sets the stage for the despair and anger that follows. The people, like the prodigal, have gone away into the foreign land. The people have refused to return (see vv. 5 and 6).

The story does not end here. Though Yahweh's child, Ephraim, shows no sign of returning, the parent, as in the Lucan parable, feels compassion. In Hosea, the compassion is born not from joy but from despair. The flood of emotion is witnessed in a string of rhetorical questionings from Yahweh:

> How can I give you up, Ephraim?
> How can I hand you over, O Israel?
> How can I make you like Admah?
> How can I treat you like Zeboiim? (v. 8 NRSV)

Can this parent let go of the child, even the child bent on turning away?

Can this parent destroy this child, as the cities of Admah and Zeboiim were once destroyed?

It is wise for the storyteller to linger here a moment, to experience the ambivalence and the ambiguity of one who has been hurt and disappointed by the one who has been loved. It is helpful for the listener to sense the incredible range of emotions wrought by such a circumstance as this—the hopelessness, the disappointment, the grief, the anger, the confusion, and the sadness. It is not difficult for us to imagine the ways that we might respond to the wayward child.

The soliloquy continues. Yahweh tells us not what he will do, but in this instance what Yahweh will *not* do to the child. As compassion restrains Yahweh, he says, "I will not execute my fierce anger; I will not again destroy Ephraim" (v. 9 NRSV). We as readers are surprised, but then again, not so surprised. We have often been jarred by the violent words of destruction that have come from the mouth of Yahweh, and we have been surprised by sudden and unexpected words of compassion. Both are part of our tradition; neither can be ignored, though at times we are sorely tempted to discard either the words of anger or those of grace.

Here, as Yahweh's heart recoils within (v. 8), the decision is not to lash out in anger, and the reason is given: "for I am God and no mortal, the Holy One in your midst, and I will not come in wrath" (v. 9 NRSV). The story invites us to ponder those times in life when our first mortal response—to lash out in revenge—might need to be tempered by Yahweh's radical compassion.

Retelling the Story

Israel is like a child to God. Sometimes God walks behind this child. When there is danger, though, God puts the child behind. If a wolf comes up behind, the child will be placed in front. When the sun is too hot, God shades the child with a cloak. When the child is hungry, God provides food, and when the child is thirsty, God offers water. When the child is too tired to go on, God picks the beloved child up and carries her. This is why Hosea employs the phrase, "They were taken upon God's arms" to describe God's loving care for Israel. (*Sefer Ha-Aggadah* 72.80)

I loved my nation. I loved my God. In my early years, Jeroboam II was king of Israel. During that time, Yahweh blessed us with prosperity. Did God's people recognize the source of their wealth? No! It seemed, in fact, that the more God gave to us the farther we pulled away. It has ever been thus with these people. The more God cherishes them, the more they reject God. That prosperity, however, would soon change. They would "sow the wind and reap the whirlwind." The results would be pain, confusion, and anarchy as Israel played the harlot with other gods.

As I loved my nation and my God, so I also loved my wife, Gomer. Gomer was a beautiful woman, much sought after—too much sought after. She was in the service of Baal, the fertility god, when I was first drawn to her. I had immediate conflicts. I was called to be a prophet of my God. She had a vocation of prostitution. My God was holy; her god was permissive, even risqué. Our worship was holy, serious, and sanctified; worship of Baal was filled with sexual revelry as a metaphor of the desired fertility of the land. It seemed an impossible relationship for the two of us, a forbidden relationship.

I sought the Lord. His message to me: "Take the harlot for a wife." She bore me three children. Each of them was named by prophetic decree with names reflecting the relationship of Israel to her Creator: a son, Jezreel—"For in a little while I am going to punish the dynasty of Jehu for the blood shed in the valley of Jezreel"; a daughter, Lo-ruhamah—"I shall never again show love to Israel, never again forgive them"; and a son, Lo-ammi—"Not my people." Tiring of life as a wife of a prophet, and mother of my children, she left, returning to her earlier profession.

I was crushed, but I saw the whole experience, as God intended, as a metaphor for his relationship with Israel. My sorrow opened my eyes, and became the basis of my message. Then spoke the Lord, and I carried his message to the people . . .

"Do you think that because I am God I cannot and do not suffer? I feel! I feel love, compassion, anger, and grief, just as you do! I am not remote and removed from you. Everyday I am involved with you; everyday I cherish memories of the past and have hope for the future.

> Israel did not say to God that ten commandments were enough. Nor would they stop at twenty, or thirty. Rather they said, "Everything that God commands we will do." (*Sefer Ha-Aggadah* 341.48)

"Memories of you, Israel, flash through my mind like a slide show at a family reunion. I loved you as a child in Egypt. I taught you to walk. I held you in my arms. When you were sick I nursed, and I healed you, but you were oblivious. I fed you. But it seems that the more I did for you, the more I called you, the more you went away from me. Memories—painful and sweet—they will not, indeed cannot, go away. Now you are in a foreign land, under the yoke of Assyria, but I won't give up on you. How can I— how could I give you up?

"Do I, must I, deal with you as I dealt with the cities of the plain that perished

> Moses told Joshua that the people who were given into his care were immature. They are like the kids of goats. Moses told the younger leader, "Don't let the things they do provoke you too much. Remember they are still very young in following the ways of God." So Hosea said, "When Israel was a youth, I loved him. Out of Egypt I called my son." (*Sefer Ha-Aggadah* 727.46)

with Sodom and Gomorrah? My love must be evenhanded. My love must be balanced with justice. Otherwise, love has no integrity. You sow and you reap. Your sins bring their own reward; but I cannot destroy you. I will bring you back. I will speak tenderly to you, allure you, and you will be my wife. You will share my life, my feelings, my love." *(Ed Thorn)*

AMOS 5:6, 10-15, 18-24; 6:1-7

The Revelry of the Loungers

One last chance for the rich, who do not yet seek the Lord.

The Story

If you would live, make your way to
the LORD,
or he will break out against Joseph's
descendants like fire,
fire which will devour Bethel with no
one to quench it.
....
you that hate a man who brings the
wrongdoer to court
and abominate him who speaks
nothing less than truth:
for all this, because you levy taxes on
the poor
and extort a tribute of grain from
them,
though you have built houses of
hewn stone,
you will not live in them;
though you have planted pleasant
vineyards,
you will not drink wine from them.
For I know how many are your
crimes,
how monstrous your sins:
you bully the innocent, extort
ransoms,
and in court push the destitute out of
the way.
In such a time, therefore, it is
prudent to stay quiet,
for it is an evil time.

Seek good, and not evil,
that you may live,
that the LORD, the God of Hosts, may
be with you,
as you claim he is.
Hate evil, and love good;
establish justice in the courts;
it may be that the LORD, the God of
Hosts,
will show favour to the survivors of
Joseph.
....
Woe betide those who long for the
day of the LORD!
What will the day of the LORD mean
for you?
It will be darkness, not light;
it will be as when someone runs
from a lion,
only to be confronted by a bear,
or as when he enters his house
and leans with his hand on the wall,
only to be bitten by a snake.
The day of the LORD is indeed
darkness, not light,
a day of gloom without a ray of
brightness.

I spurn with loathing your pilgrim-
feasts;
I take no pleasure in your sacred
ceremonies.
When you bring me your whole-
offerings and your grain-offerings
I shall not accept them,
nor pay heed to your shared-offerings
of stall-fed beasts.
Spare me the sound of your songs;

I shall not listen to the strumming of
　your lutes.
Instead let justice flow on like a river
and righteousness like a never-failing
　torrent.
....
Woe betide those living at ease in
　Zion,
and those complacent on the hill of
　Samaria,
men of mark in the first of nations,
those to whom the people of Israel
　have recourse!
Go over and look at Calneh,
travel on to great Hamath,
then go down to Gath of the
　Philistines—
are they better than these kingdoms,
or is their territory greater than
　yours?

You thrust aside all thought of the
　evil day
and hasten the reign of violence.
You loll on beds inlaid with ivory
and lounge on your couches;
you feast on lambs from the flock
and stall-fed calves;
you improvise on the lute
and like David invent musical
　instruments,
you drink wine by the bowlful
and anoint yourselves with the
　richest of oils;
but at the ruin of Joseph you feel no
　grief.
Now, therefore, you will head the
　column of exiles;
lounging and laughter will be at an
　end.

Comments on the Story

Though only parts of Amos 5 and 6 are used in the lectionary throughout the season of Pentecost, the storyteller is well advised to read the chapters in their entirety. Only then can the significant literary patterns be discerned. The most obvious pattern in chapter 5 is the repetitive use of the verb "to seek." Three times it occurs in similar, yet differing phraseology in the NRSV:

> "Seek me and live . . . " (v. 4)
> "Seek the LORD and live . . . " (v. 6)
> "Seek good and not evil that you may live;
> and so the LORD, the God of hosts, will be with you . . . " (v. 14)

While chapter 5 begins with a funeral song for the fallen Israel and is punctuated with references to destruction (v. 9), mourning, wailing, and lamentation (vv. 16-17), there is for the reader one element of hope. According to Amos 5 there is still time for the people to experience *life* if the people choose to *seek* Yahweh. "Seek and you will live," is the text's modest refrain.

A cursory reading of the chapter reveals the many transgressions of the people that will, if not reversed, bring death. The people abhor truth (v. 10), trample on the poor (v. 11), and take bribes and push aside the needy (v. 12). The general indictment in verse 7 envelops all these offenses: "Ah, you that turn justice to wormwood, and bring righteousness to the ground" (NRSV)! There is no mistaking the sins of the people or the expectations of Yahweh—both have something to do with the way people in the community treat one another. This is at the heart of the message of Amos.

The pervasive sadness in the "story" comes from the people's never really understanding the enormity of their problem or the disastrous consequences of their behaviors. They are blind to the wishes of Yahweh. Naively they expect that their encounter with Yahweh, "the day of the LORD," will be filled with light and brightness (vv. 18-20). The prophetic word is that for those who do not "seek life" the encounter is filled with darkness and gloom. That the darkness and gloom is not expected by the people of Israel is brought to life almost humorously by the prophet—"It is darkness, not light; as if someone fled from a lion, and was met by a bear; or went into the house and rested a hand against the wall, and was bitten by a snake" (v. 19 NRSV). A person fleeing from a lion would not expect to run into a bear, a person resting in her home does not expect to be bitten by a snake, and the people of Israel do not expect from Yahweh the darkness of death.

The teller continues to be plagued by the imperative commands to seek Yahweh. The commands are left ambiguous; the reader is not told how to seek the presence or the approval of Yahweh. Yet, the reader knows that life is dependent upon the search. The clue finally comes in verses 21-25. We are made aware that it is not festivals and solemn assemblies that will please Yahweh. It is not offerings—Yahweh will neither accept nor look upon them (v. 22). Yahweh is neither pleased with the noise of song nor melodious music. "But let justice roll down like waters, and righteousness like an everflowing stream" (v. 24). This is what it means to be a person of Yahweh! The Hebrew terms here suggest a river freely flowing, that never dries, filled with cascading water. That which Israel has contaminated into wormwood and poison (see 5:7) was meant to bring refreshment and blessing to the community. Just as streams were to bring the gift of life to those who live in a sometimes arid land, so the people of God were to give life through their acts of justice and righteousness to the world around them.

It is sometimes not easy for us to see ourselves reflected in the words and accusations of chapter 5. The calls to justice and righteousness are perhaps too vague, too abstract for us to grasp. If we cannot see ourselves clearly in the verses of chapter 5, perhaps chapter 6 provides the mirror in which we can see ourselves distinctly and painfully reflected. There Amos addresses those who are at ease and those who feel secure (v. 1), those who lie on beds of ivory and lounge on couches, who eat lambs and calves, who sing idle songs, who drink wine from bowls, and anoint themselves with finest oil. Amos addresses those who do not grieve over the ruin of the land (v. 6). This "revelry of the loungers" (v. 7 NRSV) Amos says, will pass away.

Those who are living the secure and luxurious life will perhaps be offended by the words of Amos for the words are a wake-up call to take seriously the disease in the world that surrounds them. We are reminded of the three-fold imperative in chapter 5: Seek! Seek! Seek! We are reminded that we are called to be doers of the word.

For those who feel trampled by the rich and who are needy but pushed aside at the city gate, perhaps these words provide a glimmer of hopefulness. As long as the prophetic words of Amos are with us, there is the slightest possibility that the conscience of the "loungers" will be pricked, and that together we will become a world that seeks and finds Yahweh's light.

Retelling the Story

He came into the quaint mountain town wearing blue jeans, and a plaid, flannel shirt—his clothes patched and old but clean. His hair was somewhat long, his beard was full. His feet were shod in sandals. He walked purposefully. No one had ever seen him before. He knocked on doors looking for work. A few kindly souls fed him in exchange for trimming hedges, replacing a rotten board on a porch, and helping some farmers shear sheep.

Others were not so kindly. They were a close-knit community in which everyone knew everyone else. Indeed, most of the town was in some way related to most of the others in town, if only in a distant way. They weren't too used to strangers. Sometimes those who came by were up to no good. It wasn't that most of the people weren't friendly and caring, but news that drifted in of the world outside was frightening. In contrast, in their town, people left their doors and windows unlocked. Things hadn't changed much for centuries.

It wasn't that they were all saints. There were whispers of corruption among the town officers. "The good old boys" kept their kinfolk happy by sheltering them from the outer world, keeping the taxes low, and by playing Santa Claus at Christmastime.

Bordering on the town's undeveloped territory was a highway. No one lived near it, but technically it was incorporated. The speed limit shifted suddenly from fifty-five to thirty-five miles per hour there, though it was scarcely noticeable since the speed limit signs were half covered with brush. When radar was first invented the town fathers realized they had a gold mine. They had the authority to raise the speed limit, but the current policy suited their convenience.

On Sunday morning, the stranger was at the Community Church. All the people that "really counted" were there, dressed in their Sunday finest. Most of them welcomed the stranger, even though he was not dressed like them. The pastor, too, welcomed him during the service, at which time the stranger said, "May I say a word?"

He had the clear resonant voice of a Shakespearean actor. He complimented the people on the safety of their town and their old-time value system. He mentioned a few other places such as Newark, Homestead, Atlanta, Covington, and Cicero. He had been in these cities, he said. People were afraid to walk the streets at night. Gangs of marauding youth fought one another with automatic weapons over tiny turfs. People were known to ingest drugs in one form or another.

The townspeople's heads nodded. This information confirmed the rumors they had heard. "Thank God there is none of that here," someone was heard to whisper.

The stranger intimated that the judgment of the Almighty was involved and would continue to be seen unless those folks repented. Amens were heard

> There was one rabbi who would weep when he read Amos. It was said that the prophet reminded him that even the most inconsequential act could lead to sin and be held against an individual by God. The words of comfort he sought were also in Amos, "Hate evil and love good; establish justice in the courts; it may be that the Lord, the God of Hosts, will show favor to the survivors of Joseph." (*Lamentations Rabbah* 3.28-30 [9] and *Leviticus Rabbah* 26.7)

throughout the sanctuary. Then the stranger unsettled them with a direct attack on some of the church's most revered leaders—prominent, respected citizens of the community. The policemen and the justice of the peace took bribes. Officers of the women's society hired illegal aliens as maids and gardeners, paying them subminimum wages, with no Social Security or medical benefits. These servants could scarcely buy shoes for their children to protect them against the freezing winter weather.

Those people who passed along the highway at the edge of town and were arrested were often the unemployed, destitute citizens of distant settlements. They looked "trashy." Consequently, they were more likely to be arrested than those driving a Cadillac or Mercedes. One had to be careful about those folk. They were often well-connected. But the beat-up old station wagons were fair game. Usually these people were just passing through, anguishing for a new start in life in a new community, only to be set upon by wheedling werewolves who took the last dregs of their substance.

"You think," the stranger said, "that you are favored by the Lord because you live in large Georgian colonial brick houses that display massive white columns supporting the roofs of the porches of your leisure. You have swimming pools and Jacuzzis purchased with your ill-gotten gains. You see no end to your prosperity. You celebrate in this beautiful sanctuary with hymns to your Creator, whose ways you do not understand. The Lord hates the music of your 100 rank pipe organ, much as you flee from the practice of a novice violinist. Your paid choir sounds flat and out of tune in the ears of the Almighty.

"Because of your socially acceptable transgressions against the love of God, the judgment of the Lord will come upon you. At that time, you will be like a man fleeing from a lion only to encounter a bear, or like a weary man who leans against the wall of his family room only to be bitten by a rattler.

" 'Seek me! Seek me'," says the Lord your God. " 'Seek good and not evil that your soul may live'." *(Ed Thorn)*

And Yahweh Relented

Amos has visions, about a surveyor's plumb and a sudden, undesirable career move.

The Story

This was what the Lord showed me: there he was standing by a wall built with the aid of a plumb-line, and he had a plumb-line in his hand. The LORD asked me, 'What do you see, Amos?' 'A plumb-line,' I answered. Then the Lord said, 'I am setting a plumb-line in the midst of my people Israel; never again shall I pardon them. The shrines of Isaac will be desolated and the sanctuaries of Israel laid waste; and sword in hand I shall rise against the house of Jeroboam.'

AMAZIAH, the priest of Bethel, reported to King Jeroboam of Israel: 'Amos has conspired against you here in the heart of Israel; the country cannot tolerate all his words. This is what he is saying: "Jeroboam will die by the sword, and the Israelites will assuredly be deported from their native land." ' To Amos himself Amaziah said, 'Seer, go away! Off with you to Judah! Earn your living and do your prophesying there. But never prophesy again at Bethel, for this is the king's sanctuary, a royal shrine.' 'I was no prophet,' Amos replied to Amaziah, 'nor was I a prophet's son; I was a herdsman and fig-grower. But the LORD took me as I followed the flock and it was the LORD who said to me, "Go and prophesy to my people Israel." So now listen to the word of the LORD. You tell me I am not to prophesy against Israel or speak out against the people of Isaac: Now these are the words of the LORD: Your wife will become a prostitute in the city, and your sons and daughters will fall by the sword. Your land will be parcelled out with a measuring line, you yourself will die in a heathen country, and Israel will be deported from their native land.'

Comments on the Story

The storyteller must divide Amos 7:7-17 into two units—verses 7-9 and verses 10-17—because of their radically different forms and functions.

Verses 7-9 report a vision Amos received from Yahweh. The vision is the third of three, and only when read in the context of the two preceding visions can the full import of the announcement be felt. The first vision reported in verses 1-3 recounts a scene in which Yahweh is forming locusts at the time when plants were sprouting. The locusts devour the land. Amos, understanding the vision to be a prediction of the judgment that will be received by Israel, says to Yahweh "O Lord GOD, forgive, I beg you" (v. 2 NRSV)! Amos intercedes on behalf of the people. Yahweh relents and says, "It shall not be" (v. 3 NRSV).

In verses 4-6, Amos witnesses in his vision Yahweh calling for a "shower of fire" that would devour and eat the land. Again the possibility of Israel's destruction moves Amos to intercede on behalf of the people, this time begging Yahweh to "cease." As before, Yahweh relents and says, "This also shall not be" (v. 6).

The first two visions in chapter 7 demonstrate the vulnerability of a God who would call individuals to prophesy, while knowing that their words could be so powerful that they would cause even God to change God's mind. We wonder, were prophets called to speak not only to humanity but also to deity? Do we witness in these verses a longing on God's part, a hopefulness that someone will intervene on the people's behalf and ask for their forgiveness?

It is in this context that verses 7-10 must be read. We become aware of the verses' meaning as we recognize the various ways in which this last vision differs from the previous two. The third vision is recounted; Yahweh is standing beside a wall with a plumb line. Amos acknowledges the plumb line, but unlike the two previous visions Amos is not the first to speak. Perhaps the meaning of the plumb line is not as evident as visions of locusts and showers of fire. It is Yahweh who speaks first, explaining the vision that Amos beholds, "See, I am setting a plumb line in the midst of my people Israel; I will never again pass them by" (v. 8 NRSV). The words of Yahweh come to closure with the promise of the desolation that is to come to Israel and the house of Jeroboam (v. 9).

Amos is silent. As readers we are left to wonder why. There is no begging by Amos that this not come to pass, no prayer on behalf of Israel's people. Has Amos realized that the sins of the people are too egregious? Is he tired of asking for pardon? Is he convinced that the people will never truly repent? Does he feel hopeless?

In the edited text, this vision that ends in a terrifying and unaltered word from Yahweh serves as the prelude to the narrative account of the meeting between Amaziah the priest of Bethel, and Amos who comes not from Israel in the north, but from Tekoa in the south. He is then an intruder in Israel, an intruder who speaks a forceful and uncompromised word threatening religious and political personalities in a land not his own. Reiterating the sentiments of the third vision—that the house of Jeroboam will die by the sword, Amos is himself exiled from the land of Israel. His presence is far too threatening. Amaziah says that the "land is not able to bear all his words" (v. 10). How powerful words can be if even the land cannot bear them! Yet, if the land cannot bear the prophetic word, the results are unbearable.

The prophetic word cannot be extinguished so easily. Amos, though threatened, or perhaps because he is threatened, speaks the word once again even more forcefully. To Amaziah he says:

> your wife shall become a prostitute;
> your sons and daughters shall fall by the sword;
> your land shall be parceled out;
> you shall die in an unclean land;
> Israel will go into exile. (see v. 17)

The five-fold threat personalizes the message of doom that Amos brings to the Israelite nation. The storyteller can understand why the leadership felt that Amos should be removed. We likewise do not like to hear words foretelling our own demise.

We are not told as we are with other prophets what Amos saw or felt when he received his call to be a prophet, though the visions just prior to this call are probably intended to shape our understanding of his mission. As a shepherd and a keeper of trees in Judah we only know that he heard a voice saying "Go, prophesy to my people Israel" (v. 15 NRSV). And he went. Those who later remembered his story must have been as amazed by his obedience and his courage as we are, because the brief account of his call (vv. 14-15) is enveloped by the three visions in chapter 7 and the fourth vision in 8:1-3. We are invited to remember that Amos was called to speak words to a land about its imminent end—words the land could not bear. We are invited to wonder if we could or if we can go and do likewise.

Retelling the Story

The stranger continued to speak to the congregation: "You think it is difficult to monitor the speed traps outside your community. You think your life is made complicated because you must seek out, hire, and supervise aliens who do the manual tasks in your luxurious homes. In a vision, the Lord our God, whom you claim you worship, allowed me to see the judgment that the Lord has prepared for you. It is the Lord's response to your unjust treatment of others.

"The Lord set before my eyes a picture of locusts that would devour your young crops as they began rising from the soil. I saw the sun grow dark as clouds of locusts flew through the air. You covered your ears with your hands to black out the whining sound of their buzzing wings. I saw the crops disappear. As for you, you wrung your hands in despair. I cried out to God to spare you. I thought you would repent of your ways. The Almighty withheld judgment, yet you did not repent.

"Then came a second vision. In it I saw a "shower of fire" threaten to consume your homes and destroy all in its path. I implored a merciful God to spare you; again the Lord relented. But you did not seek the Lord's favor.

> The sages knew prophecy by ten names. Four of those names were stern and six were gentle. The stern names were vision, pronouncement, preaching, and riddle. The gentle names were prophecy, seeing, watching, parable, metaphor, and holy spirit. They knew that prophecy was given for our benefit whatever name it traveled under. (*Sefer Ha-Aggadah* 475.69)

"Bad as it was, this was not all. In a third vision, the Lord showed me a plumb line. This time the Lord set the standard to which his people must rise. This time it was clear. Much singing, much money spent on beautiful instruments and musicians cannot impress the Lord.

"God's standards are: mercy to the suffering, justice to the citizens, and fairness to the employed. If you do not repent and toe the mark, your quaint mountain town will bring about its own destruction. Your leaders will be prosecuted and turned out of office."

The congregation shifted in their seats. They grew agitated at the words of the uninvited stranger. Almost as one, the minister, the lay-leader and the board of deacons rose up in rage, and said, "Shut up! Sit down! Better yet, leave! Go back to your own people and preach there. You'll get no money here for your unwanted and unwarranted preaching. Neither will you get an invitation to hold a revival here. You have a lot of nerve coming here to the governor's home church and making such threats! You're some kind of preacher. Go back home and earn your money among the tart-tongued riffraff whose son you are."

The stranger replied, "I am no preacher, nor am I the son of a preacher. I am a farmer and handyman. The Lord told me to come and appeal to you. But now you want me to shut up and leave. Therefore, this is what I now hear as the judgment of the Lord.

"There will be state and federal investigations. Your homes and land will be confiscated. Even your church will stand in ruins. Your political offices will be taken away, and your businesses will go bankrupt. Your sons and daughters will not find employment in the impoverished town that is to be. They will wander like many of the strangers on the highway, seeking opportunity in distant towns." (*Ed Thorn*)

Great Expectations

For seemingly trivial offenses, the Lord passes severe judgment on those who forget the poor.

The Story

THIS was what the Lord GOD showed me: it was a basket of summer fruit. 'What is that you are looking at, Amos?' he said. I answered 'A basket of ripe summer fruit.' Then the LORD said to me, 'The time is ripe for my people Israel. Never again shall I pardon them. On that day, says the Lord GOD, the palace songs will give way to lamentation: "So many corpses, flung out everywhere! Silence!" '

Listen to this, you that grind the poor and suppress the humble in the land while you say, 'When will the new moon be over so that we may sell grain? When will the sabbath be past so that we may expose our wheat for sale, giving short measure in the bushel and taking overweight in the silver, tilting the scales fraudulently, and selling the refuse of the wheat; that we may buy the weak for silver and the poor for a pair of sandals?' The Lord has sworn by the arrogance of Jacob: I shall never forget any of those activities of theirs.

Will not the earth quake on account of this?

Will not all who live on it mourn?
The whole earth will surge and
    seethe like the Nile
and subside like the river of Egypt.

On that day, says the Lord GOD,
I shall make the sun go down at
    noon
and darken the earth in broad
    daylight.
I shall turn your pilgrim-feasts into
    mourning
and all your songs into lamentation.
I shall make you all put sackcloth
    round your waists
and have everyone's head shaved.
I shall make it like mourning for an
    only son
and the end of it like a bitter day.

The time is coming, says the Lord GOD,
when I shall send famine on the land,
not hunger for bread or thirst for
    water,
but for hearing the word of the LORD.
People will stagger from sea to sea,
they will range from north to east,
in search of the word of the LORD,
but they will not find it.

Comments on the Story

Amos 8 is not comforting. Amos 8 is not hopeful. But Amos 8 is not surprising. As readers of the book of Amos we have come to expect a prophetic word that has something to do with justice. In 4:1 we hear a word directed to those who oppress the poor, who crush the needy. In 5:10-13, we hear a word directed to those who trample on the poor and push aside the needy. So the words to those who trample on the needy and bring to ruin the poor of the land (v. 4) come as no surprise.

Neither are we surprised by the harsh words of Yahweh that depict the disasters that will soon befall Israel. We have become accustomed as readers of Amos to predictions that in a time surely coming the land will tremble and those who live in the land will mourn (v. 8). These are not the first words we have read that have predicted mourning, lamentation, and bitterness (v. 10).

Chapter 8 begins by recounting the fourth vision of Amos. Yahweh shows him a basket of summer fruit; again another ordinary item was used to bring to the prophet the word for the hour. Yahweh asks Amos what he sees. He replies, "A basket of summer fruit." At this, Yahweh brings the word. "The end has come upon my people Israel; I will never again pass them by" (v. 2 NRSV).

The gravity of the situation cannot be missed. There is no call to repentance. The people are no longer called to seek Yahweh. Clearly now, the end has come. There are words related to lament and death. With an eerie imperative the vision comes to closure, "Be silent." We feel the silence, the silence that is as silent as death itself.

With these stern words, the text then turns to the indictment of Israel. The words of verse 4 are directed to those who trample on the needy and bring ruin to the poor. Their offenses are detailed in verses 5-6 and the consequences for their behaviors in verses 7-12. As readers, the disparity between the offense and the punishment amazes us. We are surprised at the *enormity* of the consequences for the unfaithfulnesses in contrast to what appears to be the *trivial* nature of the sins committed. The careful reader notes that the sins of the people are described as follows: "Hear this, you that trample on the needy, and bring to ruin the poor of the land, saying, 'When will the new moon be over so that we may sell grain; and the sabbath, so that we may offer wheat for sale? We will make the ephah small and the shekel great, and practice deceit with false balances, buying the poor for silver and the needy for a pair of sandals, and selling the sweepings of the wheat' " (vv. 4-6 NRSV).

We are *amazed*—the sins of the people are not murder, not adultery, not even the practice of idolatry. The sins are simply these: wishing for a time when the sabbath is over so that money can be made, making a dishonest deal in the marketplace, and selling not the best wheat but the "sweepings." For what seem to be minor offenses Yahweh promises that the land will mourn and darkness will cover the earth. The mourning will be like the mourning at the loss of an only son (v. 10). All because there are some unfair dealings with the poor among us? Yes! That is exactly the point Amos wants to make. Only by describing outrageous consequences for our behavior can Amos help us to see

166

the gravity of the sin. When the *most vulnerable* among us are treated unjustly—in the marketplace, in our politics, in our hearts—we have committed the most egregious offense to Yahweh.

We are called to reflect upon every part of our lives, individually and collectively, to see how the ways we live affect those who live around us. It sounds simple enough, but it is costly, so we choose not to hear the prophetic word. The time is surely coming, Yahweh says, when the people will have ignored the word for so long that though they run to and fro seeking Yahweh's word they shall not find it. The storyteller is invited to imagine a community that is desperately seeking but cannot find the word.

Retelling the Story

The stranger would not yield the floor of the church, and the church leaders near the door began to discuss ways to remove him. He continued to dissert, saying: "You have your flea markets, rummage sales, and suppers to furnish this ornate sanctuary. Your offering plates are full. You give liberally to charities and missions in far-off places, but your money is ill-gotten gain. You enlarge your bank accounts and your church treasuries through less than honorable means. In plain words, you cheat! The Lord loathes your speed traps. The Lord detests the improperly balanced scales that your merchants use. Your mechanics sabotage automobiles; they squirt oil on shock absorbers to make them appear defective when they are not. You sell the poor "new parts" for their vehicles that are already used and cleaned up in order to inflate your profits. You do not stand by your guarantees. You have no compassion on the workers who cannot pay your excessive charges on time. You repossess their jalopies, take title to them, and sell them at auction.

"You do not count your sins as significant. You brag that there is no crime in your town. Not true! Your crimes are merely different. You don't commit murder, but you take all the hope and substance you can bleed out of the poor. The Lord loathes the shacks that you provide for your migrant farm workers. Your company stores are an abomination.

"You do not wish to hear the word of the Lord. So be it! Your consciences are so calloused that you will not be able to hear the word of the Lord. Even in your time of worship, you smile at the minister, but you calculate how to make your next dollar—sometimes leaving before the final hymn so you can get on the Internet to plan your next purchase of stock before the Wall Street opening bell rings on Monday. Economically you may continue to do well, but your lives will make *Days of Our Lives* and *General Hospital* look like a Disney movie. A time of great dismay shall come upon you. You will want to hear from the Lord but your ears will so ring with the tinnitus of your offenses that you will be unable to hear the Lord speak.

"Perhaps you do not respect the word of the Lord, but do you not remember the tales you tell your little children? Do you not remember how you yourself sat at your mother's knee and learned of King Midas, the very rich king? Midas, the man with two loves in his life. One love was his daughter, Marigold. She was beautiful, sweet, kind, but also very lonely because her father seldom gave her his time. He gave her almost anything she wanted. Only one thing did he withhold: himself. He was always busy—busy at his first love, making and counting money. He had more money than almost anyone else in the world, but he was fascinated with obtaining more. Although he had so much that he would have had difficulty spending it all in one lifetime, he connived to stuff his vaults with a greater supply of gold. One day he was compulsively counting his money. He got lost in it. Time stood still for him. He was absorbed like a mystic who is one with the universe, touching infinity. Indeed, Midas was in mystical oneness with his wealth, almost oblivious to all else. Almost oblivious, but not quite. His only sorrow was his knowledge that his gold was not infinite. Suddenly, in the midst of Midas's musings there stood an angel made of shimmering light. 'How much gold would it take to complete your happiness?' queried the angel.

" 'I wish, yes, I wish that everything I touch would turn to gold.' He did not know that his wish was not wise.

" 'Your wish is granted,' the angel said with an indulgent heavenly smile.

"Midas ran about his castle touching everything, even the very walls, turning them to gold. Not content with this, he touched the trees, the bushes and the flowers around his castle. Exhausted, he

> When God speaks of turning feasts into mourning it points to the fact that none of us can foresee the end of our lives. There is a story of a man who held a feast to celebrate his son's circumcision. He told the wine steward to save back some of the wine so that he and his son might celebrate with it at the son's wedding. One of the guests on his way from the feast encountered the angel of death. When asked who he was, the angel said simply that he was a messenger of God. The guest then asked why the angel looked so strange and was told that the angel was puzzled by the way humans planned to do this and that at some future date when none knew the date they would die. The man who wanted to save wine for his son's wedding had no assurance that either he or his son would live to see that day. When the guest asked to see his time and place of death, the angel had to admit that not even he knew such things so precisely. You see, God would sometimes be gracious enough to add to an individual's span of life. (*Deuteronomy Rabbah* 9.1)

turned a newly-turned-golden doorknob, and made his way to the golden dining room with its golden furniture and golden forks. He seemed not to notice. He loved the golden gleam, oblivious to the monotony of the unbroken sameness. His favorite food was on the table: Welsh rarebit. He picked up his golden fork and touched the first bite to his lips. He crunched it with his teeth, but its golden metallic surface would not yield to his bite. That was his first clue that he had done something stupid. The second clue came momentarily, when Marigold skipped into the room and greeted her father with open arms. Before he could shriek '*no*,' she turned into a most exquisite, golden statue such as no sculptor could ever sculpt.

"Tears of remorse ran down his cheeks scattering all over the table and floor, looking for all the world like golden buckshot. Now he was able to understand true values. The angel confronted him again and gave him another wish. You remember the end of the story, but I fear for you. You will find no happy ending until you choose compassion and mercy. Then, and only then, will I rebuild your broken lives."

As the pipe organ thundered "Amazing Grace" to drown him out, the stranger departed. (*Ed Thorn*)

Torn Skin, Broken Bones

The leaders are so corrupt and full of self-interest that they boil the powerless in a cauldron and eat their flesh.

The Story

These are the words of the LORD about the prophets who lead my people astray, who promise prosperity in return for food, but declare open war against those who give them nothing to eat:

For you night will bring no vision,
darkness no divination;
the sun will go down on the
   prophets,
daytime will be blackness over them.
Seers and diviners alike will be
   overcome with shame;
they will all put their hands over
   their mouths,
for there is no answer from God.
But I am full of strength, of justice
   and power,
to declare to Jacob his crime,
to Israel his sin.
Listen to this, leaders of Jacob,
you rulers of Israel,
who abhor what is right
and pervert what is straight,
building Zion with bloodshed,
Jerusalem with iniquity.
Her leaders sell verdicts for a bribe,
her priests give rulings for payment,
her prophets practise divination for
   money,
yet claim the LORD's authority.
'Is not the LORD in our midst?' they
   say,
'No disaster can befall us.'
Therefore, because of you
Zion will become a ploughed field,
Jerusalem a heap of ruins,
and the temple mount rough
   moorland.

Comments on the Story

"Listen, you heads of Jacob and rulers of the house of Israel! Should you not know justice?" The third chapter of Micah (NRSV) begins with these words. The reader recognizes that what will follow are indictments of Israel's leadership.

Religious? Political? We do not yet know, but we will come to find out that virtually no form of leadership is immune to the harsh critique of Yahweh and prophet. With graphic metaphor the prophet describes those who, in reality, do *not* know justice—those who hate the good and love the evil (v. 2). The indictment is troubling and disconcerting; scarcely can we let our imaginations conjure pictures of torn flesh, protruding bone, broken bone, and human flesh cut and boiling in the cauldron. This startling and impassioned portrait depicting the powerful preying upon the powerless serves as the general introduction to the more specific charges found in the lectionary reading for Pentecost (vv. 5-12).

Is all leadership corrupt? That is the question that haunts the reader of Micah 3 who finds that rulers, priests, and prophets alike are scrutinized under the prophet's stern gaze. The rulers and chiefs abhor justice and pervert equity. The rulers are susceptible to bribes (v. 11). The priests teach for a price (v. 11). The prophets prophesy "peace" to those who pay them well but declare war against those who do not pay; they give oracles for money. In many prophetic texts, like the laments in Jeremiah, we witness the extreme *external* forces that come to bear upon the prophet, stifling and perhaps silencing the prophetic word. In Micah 3, however, we come to witness a different kind of stifling of truth; the *internal* longing for power that comes from within those who have authority and positions of leadership in the community. The consistent theme running through the charges levied against prophet, priest, and ruler alike is this—they can all be *bought* for a price. When their priority becomes gain for self and not justice for the community they serve, they destroy the people who depend upon them. It is as if they tear off the skin of the people, break their bones and chop them up like meat destined for the kettle. They devour them; they use them; they abuse them.

Do the leaders not know they have perverted their calls? That is what is so frightening about the third chapter of Micah. The lure to abuse one's power is seductive and, at the same time, so deceptive that the leaders are *not* aware that they have succumbed to temptation. As they devour the very people of Yahweh they say, "Surely Yahweh is with us! No harm shall come upon us!" Micah knew, just as we know, that corrupt leaders are sometimes responsible for the demise of nations and churches. We will have no difficulty thinking of numerous stories in which others let power overwhelm them. We will have more difficulty thinking of times when *we* have been "bought" for a price because the temptations are, as Micah knew, so subtle and deceptive.

These accusations against the leaders of Israel climactically bring to a close three chapters in Micah that detail the threats directed against both Samaria and Jerusalem. Immediately chapter 4 begins a collection of prophecies of Israel's magnificent future "in days to come." The prophecies are a welcome relief; yet, the first three chapters of Micah have been so convincing and we have felt so fully the demise of the nation that it is difficult for us to believe that there is for this corrupt community a glimmer of hope.

There is, however, a single foreshadowing in Micah 1–3, a single glimpse of goodness. In the midst of the prophecies Micah brought against the rulers, chiefs, prophets, and priests of Samaria and Jerusalem we read these words:

"But as for me, I am filled with power, with the spirit of the LORD, and with justice and might, to declare to Jacob his transgression and to Israel his sin" (3:8 NRSV).

Perhaps there is hopefulness for the nation if just one person who is filled with the power and the spirit and the justice and might of Yahweh speaks. We as storytellers know the tales of such women and men, girls and boys. We are, however, at first skeptical of Micah's words. Is it possible that he, too, has been deceived and seduced by his office? Does he claim to speak Yahweh's word when in reality he speaks only his own? No, probably not, because Micah is not proclaiming the "easy" word. He is speaking the difficult word—the word about transgression and the word about sin. He speaks against the highest and the mightiest, those who are established and could provide honor and security for him. He speaks the word that will enrich the life of the *whole* community; he speaks the word about justice and equality for those who are powerless. Such is the calling of the true prophet of Yahweh. Such is a nation's hope.

Retelling the Story

The freshman legislator peered around the Gothic room at her fellow legislators. How would she be received in this body of lawmakers? She knew that there were close-knit special interest groups that would try to influence her, influence each other, and indeed, influence the whole legislative body to institute laws that would enhance their own individual, political, social, and financial worlds.

Micahla felt glad and honored that the people of her district had entrusted her with the responsibility of influencing the legislature for the betterment of their district, indeed for the improvement of the entire community. But as she studied her colleagues, her heart ached within her. Micahla knew the implications of trying to change the system from within. She knew how throughout history the behavior of the career politicians was corrupted with self-interest.

The appointed chaplain was about to open the session with prayer. Tears formed in her eyes as Micahla bowed her head with the other legislators. The words of the chaplain asked for God's blessing on the coming debates of law. Micahla knew that the chaplain had been hired over other applicants by powerful legislators because he could be counted upon to exert his influence on members of the religious community. They expected him to enlist support for the passing of laws that appeared to enhance the economy of the nation, but often did so at the expense of the poor, the family, and the middle class. Always a bill's worth, or worthlessness, was measured with regard to how it enhanced a legislator's own district.

As the chaplain's voice sonorously intoned "Amen and Amen," Micahla's eyes scanned the body of lawmakers. She looked at the men and women of the group who had claimed that they felt the vocation of politics was a call from the Creator. They said, as with one voice, that they were carrying out God's will to preserve the nation as a bastion of truth, liberty, and justice. But during their time in office, these representatives of the people had used their positions to line their own pockets with money, provide their relatives with jobs, and travel to exotic parts of the world at government expense, while dining sumptuously with lobbyists.

Micahla wept. Where was the glory of the calling to service? Where was the integrity of high office she had imagined as a novice legislator? Where was the voice of God to be heard? She was aware that her predecessor resigned at the end of his term saying it was hopeless. He no longer felt he could make an impact on bureaucrats, political hacks, and career politicians. Could she, as one person, influence this governing body for the good of the people? Could she resist the seductive voices of the purveyors of "pork barrel profiteering"? How?

> The sages were always finding connection between seemingly unrelated passages of scripture. Some rabbis say that the plowed field that Zion will become was actually a reference to the field in which Cain killed Abel. They suggest that the argument that led to Abel's death began over which of Adam and Eve's sons would provide the parcel of land on which the Temple would be built generations later. That is how the deadly field of Genesis and the plowed field of Micah are related. (*Genesis Rabbah* 22.7)

Her colleagues looked at her tears with contempt, believing her to be starry-eyed, weak, and an easy mark; one who would soon follow their "form of justice." Micahla closed her eyes, her spirit soaring as she prayed, "But as for me, I am filled with power, with the Spirit of the LORD, and with justice and might. . . . Surely," she mused, "the presence of the Lord is in this place."

Micahla pondered the future in her heart. She felt her weaknesses profoundly. But she knew, as others who had gone before her knew, that the only thing needed for evil people to triumph was for good people to do nothing. Micahla was beginning to see the direction her service would take. She would prayerfully accept the challenge. (*Ed Thorn*)

And They Shall Live Secure

A ruler from Bethlehem will rise up to lead Israel out of oppression.

The Story

B ut from you, Bethlehem in
Ephrathah,
small as you are among Judah's
clans,
from you will come a king for me
over Israel,
one whose origins are far back in the
past, in ancient times.
Therefore only until she who is
pregnant has given birth
will he give up Israel;
and then those of the people that
survive
will rejoin their brethren.
He will rise up to lead them
in the strength of the LORD,
in the majesty of the name of the
LORD his God.
They will enjoy security, for then his
greatness will reach
to the ends of the earth.
Then there will be peace.

Comments on the Story

Micah 5:2-5*a* is centered in two chapters, a collection of prophecies that
describe the wonderful and glorious future of Zion. These two chapters
describe a day when the community will beat its swords into plowshares and
spears into pruning hooks, a day when there will be no more war (4:3). This
day that is to come will be a day when no one will be afraid (4:4). Micah 5:2-
5*a* itself speaks of a time when a new kind of ruler will come forth out of one
of the small clans in Judah.

It is not surprising that this particular text should find its way into the lectionary on the fourth Sunday of Advent. It speaks of Bethlehem, of a woman in
labor giving birth, of a child who shall eventually stand and feed the flock in
the strength of the Lord, of one who will be great to the ends of the earth, one
of peace. Certainly the author of the Gospel of Matthew thought that in his day
these words could be used to describe the infant Jesus who had been sent to
shepherd Israel (Matt. 2:6).

This unit follows a difficult verse (5:1) that in all probability speaks to a
nation that is in great distress; larger political forces are threatening its very
survival. The focus is on one who comes from Bethlehem of Ephrathah (a clan
of people living in the area). In contrast to the great Jerusalem that, according
to Micah, is now doomed, Bethlehem was "one of the little clans of Judah"

(v. 2 NRSV). It was also, however, the home of Jesse, David's father. The ruler coming from Bethlehem is consistent with what we have come to expect from Old Testament narrative. God chooses the least likely, the smallest, to accomplish God's purpose. God will choose one from the small village of Bethlehem to bring peace. The one who comes will be like a shepherd and his fame will be to the ends of the earth (v. 4). He shall be one of peace.

Some scholars believe that this text is not original to Micah, that perhaps it was added to the more somber and sobering words of chapters 1–3 in the exilic or post-exilic period when the community was anticipating the restoration of the then fallen Davidic dynasty. Some believe that this hopeful song belongs to the time of Micah itself, that in the midst of the great despair Micah was able to "lift his eyes" and see beyond what was to what some day would be.

The historical questions surrounding this text in Micah can never be definitively settled; we can never know with certainty when the words were spoken or penned. We do know, however, that the words *could* have been written at most any time and in most any community. Communities like Matthew's, or like ours, each with its own political turmoil and upheaval, have been willing to adopt these words and claim them as their own because they speak to a longing that we have, a longing for ourselves and for the communities in which we live. The storyteller will be able to bring to her own community a story that depicts this profound longing; it is a longing for security and for peace. And perhaps the storyteller will also be able to bring tales about peace and security that have come from insignificant, small, and surprising places.

Retelling the Story

The early months of her term rolled by. Micahla observed much, even as she herself was being observed. Many smiled at her naive idealism. The jaundiced, experienced legislators had seen it before, well-meaning neophytes who eventually became cynical like themselves. They often became the biggest "takers" among the body. "Give her time," the critics droned.

Micahla, in the meantime, was aghast at the information she received. Letters, phone calls, and personal contacts glaringly pointed the finger at unresponsive bureaucracies as well as industrial leaders who, in cost-cutting moves, fired employees who had served them well for decades. Micahla soon learned of blatant racism in juries who would not convict those of their own race when there was a crime perpetrated on the citizens of another race. Indeed the justice system seemed in turmoil. Neither the defense nor the prosecution seemed interested in guilt or innocence. Their objective was merely to win. To accomplish their objectives, attorneys deliberately filled the jury boxes with the ignorant, the unlettered, and the unaware. Worse yet, the rich could afford teams of lawyers who obfuscated the issues. These rich clients were able to go free, seemingly unaccountable for murder, mayhem, rape, and fraud. As a response to this "system," it was not unknown among the police to manufacture evidence to "assure justice."

It wasn't only the courts that were corrupt; church leaders used their positions to fleece the widows, even using Ponzi, or pyramid schemes. Elsewhere international leaders continued to build war machines. Fratricidal warfare split nations in two. Ethnic and religious cleansing seemed to be the order of the day.

Micahla's chief committee assignment was to "Foreign Relations." The big issue at the moment was involvement in The League. The League was an international diplomatic force for peacekeeping. She loved the concept, but it seemed at times to be little more than a propaganda arm for the different nations of its constituency. The next evening at a reception, she would address representatives of that body. Normally, the task would have fallen to a more senior member of the Foreign Relations Committee, but her jaundiced colleagues sought to exploit Micahla's idealistic naiveté.

Perhaps, they reasoned, a fresh voice of one not so easily stereotyped and laden with the baggage of the past might draw the old curmudgeons closer. Micahla may have been idealistic, but she was not as naive as her colleagues assumed. She was keenly aware of the self-serving depravity and divisiveness within her nation, and among other international entities.

She was working late on her speech, but getting nowhere, when through the mists of her mind, she overheard Christmas carols in the distance. Where was the justice and peace heralded in those hymns that was the common hope of all people? Would there never be an end to this distrust and divisiveness? She wanted to make a difference, but could she? Could anyone? She put aside her labor to retire. Sleep did not come easily, however, and when it did, it was troubled. In her dreams, she kept writing and rewriting her speech. In one dream, she was being introduced at the podium; her hair was in shambles; her dress was tattered and immodest, and she still hadn't composed a speech. She had no idea what to say. The scene changed. She was in a far off land, in a different time, listening to the speech of a swarthy, bearded prophet who seemed to be addressing a body of leaders who were also facing an international crisis. His words seemed vaguely familiar.

"These are times like that of a pregnant woman about to go into labor. When her time comes to fruition, the nations will turn to the house of God. Fear will disappear as men and nations beat their swords into ploughshares and their spears into pruning hooks. Nations will not lift up swords against nation; they shall not learn war anymore. . . . In tiny Bethlehem shall come forth a divinely anointed leader of eternal origin. He shall bring peace to all nations."

The scene changed again. Micahla stood outside of a tall building she knew to be The League headquarters and saw written over the doorway the very words of the prophet: "They shall beat their swords into ploughshares."

She woke up with hope, not a program for peace, but a hope—a hope shared by inspired leaders who had heard the ancient dream, the heartbeat of mankind. She would appeal to that hope. She would tell them to keep the faith. She knew her Maker had placed that hope in the hearts of all peoples. As they focused on the dream, instead of just the differences between them, hope could be kept alive for a day when those differences no longer would be settled by belligerent means. The Lord God would provide the leadership. *(Ed Thorn)*

Israel's greatness is compared by the sages to a pregnant woman. If the woman gives birth before the time is right, the child will not survive. On the other hand, if the woman gives birth when the time is right for the child to be born, then it will live. Just so when Israel waits for the fullness of time, God's time, then what God has planned will be brought to birth. That is why the prophet Micah wrote, "She who was pregnant has given birth." (*Song of Songs Rabbah* 8.14 [1])

As Easy as 1, 2, 3

Instead of sacrifices and gifts, God asks for kindness, justice, and humility.

The Story

HEAR what the LORD is saying:

Stand up and state your case
  before the mountains;
let the hills hear your plea.
Hear the LORD's case, you
  mountains;
listen, you pillars that support the
  earth,
for the LORD has a case against his
  people,
and will argue it with Israel.

My people, what have I done to
  you?
How have I wearied you? Bring your
  charges!
I brought you up from Egypt,
I set you free from the land of
  slavery,
I sent Moses, Aaron, and Miriam to
  lead you.
My people, remember the plans
devised by King Balak of Moab,
and how Balaam son of Beor
  answered him;

consider the crossing from Shittim to
  Gilgal,
so that you may know the victories
  of the LORD.

What shall I bring when I come
  before the LORD,
when I bow before God on high?
Am I to come before him with
  whole-offerings,
with yearling calves?
Will the LORD be pleased with
  thousands of rams
or ten thousand rivers of oil?
Shall I offer my eldest son for my
  wrongdoing,
my child for the sin I have
  committed?

The LORD has told you mortals what is
  good,
and what it is that the LORD requires
  of you:
only to act justly, to love loyalty,
to walk humbly with your God.

Comments on the Story

What do you want from me? It is not difficult for the contemporary story-teller to think of a variety of times and places when one person asks this question of another. Children ask parents. Parents ask children. Friend asks friend. Spouse asks spouse. Partner asks partner. And throughout the ages in a multitude of languages and all over the world, people have asked the question of

God. What is it that you really want from me? Perhaps it is a question never fully answered, that is, never fully answered for all time. Individuals and communities who find an answer for today, often find themselves flung into the search again in the tomorrow because, though the question remains the same, the answer seems evasive and elusive.

It is that question—What do you want from me?—that Micah 6:6-8 sets out to answer. The worshiper, in verse 6, begins by asking one question with two parallel parts. "With what shall I come before the LORD, and bow myself before God on high" (NRSV)? The worshiper continues by trying to answer his own question with another. Should I bring a year old calf? That would be, of course, the normal offering that one would bring to Yahweh. But is that what Yahweh really wants? Perhaps the normal offering is not enough, so the worshiper considers offering a greater sacrifice, an abnormally generous one—thousands of rams, ten thousands of rivers of oil. Anything and everything this worshiper would consider bringing to Yahweh. No, perhaps that is not even enough—should I bring, the worshiper wonders, my own child for sacrifice? Would that please Yahweh? In his mind the worshiper has traveled from the ordinary to the extraordinary—simply trying to answer the question—What, Yahweh, do you want from me?

In its present context verses 6-8 are attached to Micah 6:1-5 where, using the imagery of the court of law, the prophet sets out for the reader the picture of a disappointed and disillusioned God who has a controversy with the people of the land. Yahweh recounts the story of salvation experienced by their ancestors in Egypt and how Moses and Aaron and Miriam were sent before them, and how they were redeemed. The storyteller can pause here to remind the listeners of the wondrous act of deliverance that occurred as the Israelites were led out from bondage. They can be invited to remember, as was Micah's audience, the courage and the despair of the reluctant Moses, the support of his brother Aaron, and the courageous questioning of Miriam who would at one time sing a glorious song of victory and at another time stand outside the camp stricken with leprosy because she knew in her heart that she, too, could be a spokesperson for Yahweh. Do you not know the story, Yahweh was asking them? Have you not heard about my saving acts? Do you not yet know how to be my people?

Our worshiper does not seem to know. The sacrifice of the flocks of rams, the rivers of oil, even the giving of the child—that is not what Yahweh wants. Yahweh wants justice, kindness, and someone who will walk humbly alongside God. It is deceptively simple, this one, two, three. It is embracing

justice—preserving the rights of all in the community;
kindness—to love in God's timeless and unconditional way; and
a humble walk—to be aware of one's need for God who walks as a partner
        throughout life.

Is it possible, we wonder, to be that committed, that inclusive, that loving? As we read this injunction we become aware, almost painfully, that God does not want what we own. God wants who we are or, at least, God wants the world to see whose we are.

Perhaps when we cry out to God—What do you want from us?—we already know the answer. We almost wish there was no answer, or we wish the answer wasn't quite so simple. And we wish that living out the very simple answer was not quite so difficult. It would be easier to head for the hills and bring back the flock of a thousand rams for sacrifice—even now that seems to be the easier alternative.

Retelling the Story

Micahla returned late to her apartment after her speech at the reception for the international League leaders. People had been polite to her. That was the nature of such receptions, particularly with a strong contingent of diplomats. She had no doubt that many thought of her as a starry-eyed idealist. She was not so out of touch with reality that she herself couldn't recognize the truth of it. She had no time to contemplate that any further, however. She was exhausted but somewhat exhilarated at the message that she deeply believed came from the Omniscient One, whatever "they" might be saying about her.

Hope, a dream to cling to, must not be forgotten, whatever the indignities and details of the human condition. The alternative was cynicism. That was no option. She would continue to look forward to a time when divine leadership should cause people to beat their ploughshares into pruning hooks.

She recognized that she had no agenda for that, only a goal, but she went to bed and slept like a child. For the first time in years she slept through her alarm, awakening only when the sun's rays peered through the window and warmed her cheeks. It was late. She hurriedly got dressed and dashed to her duties at the assembly, just a trifle late. The place seemed abuzz with whispers and glances her way as the speaker called her to the podium.

"What's this all about?" she asked.

"You are something of a celebrity," her colleagues said. "The networks have picked up excerpts of your speech. They liked it. They say you represent a fresh force to be reckoned with." There was applause from both sides of the aisle as they related to her how leaders of nation-states that no longer gave thought to the divine in human life were stirred to remember the prophetic hope. "Those of different, even opposing religious beliefs in nation-states where their traditions are deeply and tenaciously inculcated into the fiber of their laws, have endorsed your idealism, surprisingly so, since the females in many of their nations are forbidden to participate in most elements of public life."

Then one of an ethnic minority stood up and said, "We have long felt a heaviness in our spirits at the misuse and abuse of power, at the divisiveness that haunts the national and international scene. We've justified ourselves in light of conditions, and have, at least mentally, treated other factions as "the enemy." We have given up negotiations too easily. Indeed, we have played political games that purposely entrapped others. Now you stand in the tradition of one of our great prophets of the lost generation, who dreamed of a day when people will not be judged by external labels or characteristics, who dreamed of a day when people would not be judged by such as 'the color of their skin, but by the content of their character.' Micahla, I extend my hand to you. What can we expect next? Where do we go from here?"

Micahla was not used to being in the limelight. She also knew that the spotlight was fickle, but she rose to the occasion. "What next?" she asked. "Only this, know that my hand is also extended to you. Know that all of the collective rhetoric and oratory—yours, mine and ours—can and will be useless if there is not honesty and justice in the national and international scene. People are tired of politics as usual. Neither they, nor our God, will be impressed with our sacrificial hours of speaking platitudes and playing political games. We face enormous crises. The people expect leadership. They expect us, the leaders not only of this body but of the institutions of our society—especially those spiritually-based institutions—to model character they can look up to. They want heroes again. If I may turn again to the ancient prophet who inspired my speech of last evening, I would hear his words echoing in this hall. 'He—your Creator—has shown you, my people, what is good and what he requires: to act with justice, yet to love mercy and to walk humbly with your God.' " *(Ed Thorn)*

> Isaiah summarized the six hundred thirteen commandments in six principles. Micah, however, boiled all six hundred thirteen down to half that many: do justice, love kindness, and walk humbly with God. If everyone's life way is guided by these three rules, then the many commandments will flow very naturally from them. (*Sefer Ha-Aggadah* 463.567)

Asking the Right Questions

In great despair, the prophet pleads with the Lord for justice.

The Story

AN oracle which the prophet Habakkuk received in a vision.

HOW LONG, LORD, will you be deaf to my plea?
'Violence!' I cry out to you,
but you do not come to the rescue.
Why do you let me look on such wickedness,
why let me see such wrongdoing?
Havoc and violence confront me,
strife breaks out, discord arises.
Therefore law becomes ineffective,
and justice is defeated;
the wicked hem in the righteous,
so that justice is perverted.

....

I shall stand at my post,

I shall take up my position on the watch-tower,
keeping a look-out to learn what he says to me,
how he responds to my complaint.
The LORD gives me this answer:
Write down a vision, inscribe it clearly on tablets,
so that it may be read at a glance.
There is still a vision for the appointed time;
it will testify to the destined hour and will not prove false.
Though it delays, wait for it,
for it will surely come before too long.
The reckless will lack an assured future,
while the righteous will live by being faithful.

Comments on the Story

Many a good story is built not around the right answers but around the right questions. Such is the case for the prophecies of Habakkuk. This prophet asks good questions; amazingly, this prophet asks our questions.

In chapters 1 and 2 the prophet asks two series of questions (1:1-4; 1:12-17); twice Yahweh replies (1:5-11; 2:1-4). There appears to be a remarkable congruency between the two readings. Both deal with the alarming reality that the wicked in the world appear to be prosperous. How can this be when God is known to be a just God?

We know very little about the prophet Habakkuk. The usual preliminaries of the other prophetic books are here disregarded. There is simply an announcement that what will follow is the word that the prophet saw. The words are not introduced with the typical messenger formula, "Thus says the Lord." Rather, the first words, reminiscent of those found in the psalms of lament, are addressed to Yahweh as Habakkuk gives voice to an ardent and desperate prayer, "O LORD, how long shall I cry for help, and you will not listen" (1:2 NRSV)? Whatever the issue, the prophet feels abandoned. Yahweh does not listen, and Yahweh does not save (v. 2). Though many religious traditions stifle these heart-wrenching questions in corporate worship, the contemporary storyteller and her listeners can perhaps remember many times when these words from Habakkuk were words from their own hearts and souls. "How long shall I cry for help?" The prophet, now living in a time of destruction and violence, strife and contention, is consumed with his own despair. He has observed that the wicked have control over the righteous. His cry rings out, "How long?" This same sentiment is repeated in the second series of questions from the prophet to Yahweh "Why do you look on the treacherous, and are silent when the wicked swallow those more righteous than they" (1:13 NRSV)? It is an ancient question that Habakkuk asks—that the world continues to ask—a question that takes many forms: Why do the wicked prosper? What is the relationship between right behavior and prosperity in this life? Why does God allow the good to be "swallowed" by the wicked? Does God not hear the cries of those who suffer and who are afflicted with violence and destruction? Is there any reward for faithfulness?

The questions haunt Habakkuk. And yet, he seems certain as he gives them voice that Yahweh will answer his complaint. (See 1:5-11 for the first answer that concerns the fierce and dreaded Babylonians.) As chapter 2 opens, the prophet declares that he will stand at the watchpost and will keep vigil to see what Yahweh will answer. He is not disappointed. Yahweh tells him to write the vision on tablets, write it so clearly that a runner can read it as he passes by. What Yahweh says will come to pass, will surely come to pass, though the prophet may need to wait for it.

The answer is forthcoming. "Look at the proud! Their spirit is not right in them, but the righteous live by their faith" (v. 4 NRSV). The reader wonders if Habakkuk was satisfied with this answer. The answer seems too mystifying, too ambiguous, too obscure. Chapter 2 continues, "Moreover, wealth is treacherous; the arrogant do not endure" (v. 5 NRSV). Was that answer enough? Perhaps it was enough for Habakkuk who was relieved that the answer seemed to imply that God was in control of the world, chaotic though it seemed. Perhaps Habakkuk was relieved to know that some way and some day the wicked would receive their just reward. Was that enough for Habakkuk? For us? Or do the questions about evil in this world still linger—elusive and frustratingly out of our grasp? Can we still live with a strong and tenacious inner commitment to God even in the midst of the confusing and troubling world around us?

Habakkuk is an important prophet though his words remain vaguely unfamiliar to most readers of the Old Testament. He demonstrates for us a different yet important element in the prophetic vocation. We are accustomed to reading in the pre-exilic prophets indictment after indictment of the Israelite peoples, announcements of the coming destruction wrought by the hand of Yahweh, and occasionally surprising and glorious accounts of the restoration and redemption that will be brought about in the days to come. But here, in the first two chapters of Habakkuk we have prominently displayed for us another role of the prophet—that of asking the very difficult question—of asking *God* the very difficult question, and then with single focus waiting and watching for the answer. It is an important part of being a prophet, this waiting and watching for a word from God. Habakkuk was watching for a word for his community. We wonder, *who* is watching for us?

Habakkuk 2 includes a list of five woes directed against the Babylonians; chapter 3 is a grand and glorious prayer of thanksgiving and rejoicing complete with liturgical rubrics for the Israelite worshiper. In three distinct genres, this prophetic book struggles with the same concerns about violence, the lack of justice in the world, and the saving power of Yahweh. As we read these chapters, we cannot completely relinquish the haunting realities of Habakkuk's life and our own and the agonizing questions that life leads us to ask. Like many a wonderful sermon we are drawn to this book of the Old Testament, not because it gives us answers, but because it asks our questions. There is something wonderfully freeing, even redemptive, about having our own questions brought before God.

Retelling the Story

The following is an old European/Eurasian folktale. It is here somewhat modified to emphasize Habakkuk's words (2:4 NRSV), "The righteous live by their faith."

Once upon a time in a faraway land, there was a king who ruled as righteously and lovingly as he knew how. To make sure his subjects were doing well, he would disguise himself and travel among them. That way people would not put on a false front for him.

One evening the king happened to notice a house with open doors and windows, in which a man was singing with great volume at the same time he was eating. The king knocked on the door and asked if he might come in.

"Please come in," the man said. "A guest is a gift of God."

As the disguised king ate, he asked the man about his occupation. The man replied, "I am a cobbler. The Lord blesses me with some coins each day that I spend on my supper, for which I give thanks."

"That's all you earn?" asked the king. "Just enough for tonight's meal? What about tomorrow?"

"It's all in the hands of the Lord," he said. "The Lord will provide."

The king decided to test the cobbler. *Is it possible that one can really trust his Creator so much?* he asked himself. *Tomorrow I'll pass a law forbidding shoe repair without a license. I'll see then if he really has so much faith.*

The next evening the king returned to the cobbler's house. The cobbler was his same cheery self. The king asked him how his day had gone, to which the cobbler guilelessly replied, "Our great king has proclaimed that a permit must be obtained for the repair of shoes. Today I helped people carry water from the town well to their homes. Those who could, and were of a generous nature, gave me coins with which I bought dinner. Come share it with me."

"What will you do if you make no money tomorrow drawing water?" asked the king.

"God will provide," the cobbler assured him.

The king then issued an edict that each person must draw and carry his or her own water. When the disguised king returned to the peasant's house that night, he asked how he fared in light of the king's edict.

"I chopped wood today, and I sold the wood and bought this food," the faithful peasant said. "Tomorrow if something happens, God will provide in another way."

As you might have guessed, the next day the king sent out a proclamation. This time he demanded that all woodcutters report to the palace to work. They worked all day, but were given no wages. That evening the cobbler-turned-woodcutter journeyed home. He stopped at the pawnshop and pawned his sword. He bought food. He also

The rabbis told of a king who threw a banquet and invited all of his guests to bring something to sit on. Some brought pillows, others brought mats. Still others brought rugs and mattresses. Some even came with logs and stones, as if they had neglected to think of what to bring until the last minute. When all of his guests had arrived, he asked them to be seated on whatever they had brought. The ones who had brought the logs and stones complained that their seats were uncomfortable and it was beneath them to sit on such things. The king replied, "You criticize me for the comfort of the seats you yourselves brought. Do you expect me to make my other guests sit on the rough seats you brought? If you are uncomfortable and humiliated by sitting on these seats, then you are responsible for your own humiliation." Just so God says to those who have set snares for others and fallen into the snares themselves, "You criticize me for the situations you yourselves have created?" And to those who are in Gehenna, God says, "During your lives didn't you sow the seed of gossip, scandal, and hatred? Now you are sitting in the midst of the harvest you planted." (*Ecclesiastes Rabbah* 3.9 [1]) carved a wooden blade for his sheath. That evening the king came. He asked the cobbler what he would do if there was a sword inspection on the morrow. The simple man of simple faith gave his usual answer, "God will provide."

The next morning the cobbler was told that he was to be the executioner of a prisoner. The cobbler protested that he could never do that. He was told, "You have no choice."

As the prisoner knelt before him, the cobbler prayed in a loud voice, "Almighty God, you know whether or not this man is guilty. You be his judge. If he is guilty, let my sword be sharp; if innocent, let this sword be made of wood." He dramatically drew it from his sheath, and all the people exclaimed, "It is wood. It is wooden. The man is innocent!"

The king who had set it all up, and who watched from a distance, came forward to his friend, and said, "From now on you will be my permanent guest. Now what do you think of that?"

"Wonderful," exclaimed the cobbler. "God provides."

That night the king read the words of the prophet Habakkuk, and for the first time he clearly understood that "the righteous live by their faith." *(Ed Thorn)*

One Story?

The mighty warrior God dispenses wrath to enemies and keeps God's people safe.

The Story

THIS is the word of the LORD which came to Zephaniah son of Cushi, son of Gedaliah, son of Amariah, son of Hezekiah, when Josiah son of Amon was king of Judah.

I SHALL utterly destroy everything
from the face of the earth,
says the LORD.
I shall destroy human beings and
    animals,
the birds of the air and the fish in the
    sea.
I shall bring the wicked to their
    knees
and wipe out all people from the
    earth.
This is the word of the LORD.

I shall stretch my hand over Judah,
over all who live in Jerusalem.
I shall wipe out from that place the
    last remnant of Baal,
every memory of the heathen priests,
those who bow down on the
    housetops
to the host of heaven,
those who swear by Milcom,
who have turned their backs on the
    LORD,
who have neither sought for the LORD
    nor consulted him.
Keep silent in the presence of the
    Lord GOD,
for the day of the LORD is near.

The LORD has prepared a sacrifice
and set apart those he has invited.
....
At that time
I shall search Jerusalem by lantern-
    light
and punish all who are ruined by
    complacency
like wine left on its lees,
who say to themselves,
'The LORD will do nothing, neither
    good nor bad.'
Their wealth will be plundered,
their houses laid in ruins;
they will build houses but not live in
    them,
they will plant vineyards but not
    drink the wine.

The great day of the LORD is near,
near and coming fast;
no runner is so swift as that day,
no warrior so fleet.
That day is a day of wrath,
a day of anguish and torment,
a day of destruction and devastation,
a day of darkness and gloom,
a day of cloud and dense fog,
a day of trumpet-blasts and battle
    cries
against the fortified cities and lofty
    bastions.
I shall bring dire distress on the
    people;
they will walk like the blind

because of their sin against the LORD.
Their blood will be poured out like
   dust
and their bowels like dung;
neither their silver nor their gold
will avail to save them.
On the day of the LORD's wrath
by the fire of his jealousy
the whole land will be consumed;
for he will make a sudden and
   terrible end
of all who live in the land.
....

Zion, cry out for joy;
raise the shout of triumph, Israel;
be glad, rejoice with all your heart,
daughter of Jerusalem!
The LORD has averted your
   punishment,
he has swept away your foes.
Israel, the LORD is among you as
   king;
never again need you fear disaster.

On that day this must be the
   message to Jerusalem:
Fear not, Zion, let not your hands
   hang limp.

The LORD your God is in your midst,
a warrior who will keep you safe.
He will rejoice over you and be glad;
he will show you his love once more;
he will exult over you with a shout
   of joy
as on a festal day.

I shall take away your cries of woe
and you will no longer endure
   reproach.
When that time comes;
I shall deal with all who oppress you;
I shall rescue the lost and gather the
   dispersed.
I shall win for my people praise and
   renown
throughout the whole world.
When that time comes I shall gather
   you
and bring you home.
I shall win you renown and praise
among all the peoples of the earth,
when I restore your fortunes before
   your eyes.
It is the LORD who speaks.

Comments on the Story

For many decades, nearly half a century, there was silence, and according to our biblical record no prophet came forth to speak the "word of the Lord." During this period Judah went through one of its most stormy and problematic periods of history. Manasseh was king, and he was one of the most evil rulers to sit on Judah's throne. It was when Josiah came to rule that the "word" came to the prophet Zephaniah. His concern? While the importance of justice and righteousness are clearly present as they have been with other pre-exilic prophets, Zephaniah is also concerned with cultic purity; God demands purity from God's people.

With no introduction to soften the harsh and severe word, the first verses of Zephaniah announce the threat of destruction for all the earth. These verses systematically describe the sweeping away of all animal and human life; everything upon the face of the earth will be destroyed. Zephaniah declares that the "day of the Lord" is at hand. The "day of the Lord" is a repetitive and forma-tive feature of the work.

Verses 12-18 describe those for whom Yahweh will be looking on the dreaded day. The storyteller will have no difficulty graphically depicting those cast under Yahweh's scrutinizing glare—those who take no action (thicken), those who say that Yahweh will do no good or harm. The storyteller will have no difficulty thinking of those places in our lives and in our communities where such apathy dwells. For Zephaniah these dwell in the wealthy; their houses will be laid waste. The list of adjectives and nouns in the verses that follow intentionally leave no room for the imagination; clearly they depict in unmistakable terms the coming fortunes for the Judean people: wrath, distress, anguish, ruin, devastation, darkness, and gloom. The imagery reinforces both the immensity of the devastation *and* the urgency of the message that Zephani-ah speaks. There is no time for niceties. No time for conditional speech. The day is coming, the day of the full and terrible end (v. 18). The storyteller will want to ask—When have we seen a person speak so intensely and with such a fierce energy? What issues call a person to rise up and speak such an uncom-promising and pressing word? This word about the end that is sure to come ushers in a call to repentance (2:1-3). Those who seek Yahweh, seek righteous-ness, and seek humility—*perhaps* those will be hidden on the day of wrath.

This word about the day of Yahweh and the universal destruction is not the last word from Zephaniah. Chapter 3:14-20 is used as a reading at the Easter vigil and during Advent, no doubt because of its celebratory nature and its clear affirmations of forgiveness, deliverance, strength, victory, salvation, praise, homecoming, and restoration. The rich imagery of the text provides numerous seeds from which stories can grow. Imagine a people who no longer fear disaster, or the enormous relief that is experienced when shame is changed to praise. Imagine the wonder of the gathering when all are brought home or the excitement that comes with restored fortune. This text itself comes at the end of a larger unit—a woe oracle that pronounces judgment upon the wicked city of Jerusalem (see 3:1). The city has listened to no one and has not trusted in Yahweh. Indictments are listed for the officials and leaders of the city—political and religious alike. As a result, devastation will come. Nations who watch it will be converted. A remnant will remain (see vv. 6-12). Importantly for Zephaniah those who remain will be purified and they will call upon Yah-weh's name (v. 9).

To that soiled, defiled, and oppressing city comes the final word of glorious restoration in 3:14-20. Restoration comes about through the efforts of Yahweh, the king and warrior. Victory belongs to Yahweh who will remove disaster from the communion of Zion. Yahweh will save them, redeem them, bring them home and renew their fortunes in the eyes of the world.

In Zephaniah 1 and 3 we witness in microcosm the complexity of the prophetic word. Do we as readers hold together as *one story* the uncompromising word of wrath, distress, anguish, ruin, devastation, darkness, and gloom in chapter 1 with the uncompromising word of forgiveness, deliverance, strength, victory, salvation, praise, homecoming, and restoration in chapter 3? In Zephaniah these words are bound together through the image of the warrior God who, at the same time, is the one who destroys and the one who saves.

Perhaps it is time for the storyteller to take the story we find in Zephaniah and wrap it in new metaphor—one that can still affirm the radical expectations God has for the people of God and one that still affirms God's love and redemption for the faithless. Must that story be couched in the language of devastation, military victory, and conquest? Can we find words that neither feed nor legitimate the violent in and among us? Surely we must try.

Retelling the Story

The Russians are coming! The Russians are coming! You've heard that one before, haven't you? We called them the Scythians. The God whom you worship has, for the moment, tamed that bear. Though they were a threat to us for almost one hundred years, in the long run these aggressors were only a blip on our own horizon. Thanks be to the God of our fathers—Abraham, Jacob, and David—our hearts did not fail us in this time of Scythian aggression. When our enemy gobbled up our neighbors we wondered, however, if we were next. They were but one of many nations that were a threat to us during my lifetime.

During the time of my great-grandfather, Hezekiah, a great and godly king, the Assyrians swooped down, destroyed Israel, and made Judea a subject nation. You think you have taxes! As vassals of the Assyrians, my grandfather was forced to give all the gold and silver in his palace to the Assyrians, even stripping the Temple of its gold—and that was still not enough for the Assyrian king.

When my great-grandfather, Hezekiah, died, his son, Manasseh, came to the throne. My grandfather, Manasseh, who died when I was only six, was as wicked and idolatrous as Hezekiah was good. To please the Assyrian masters, he adopted their gods. He reveled in Assyrian sovereignty, and of course was handsomely rewarded for this cooperation with these pagans. He worshiped the sun, the moon, the stars, Baal, and Ashterof. He even followed their ritual of child sacrifice and filled Jerusalem with innocent blood. He sacrificially burned his own son to appease these gods who lived only in pagan fantasy. I hate to admit it, but these times under the rulership of my grandfather, Manasseh, were the darkest moments of our nation's history.

My father, Amon, succeeded him and did nothing to bring reform. After only two years as king, there was a coup. I was left an orphan. At the age of eight I became king, but under the tutelage of Hilkiah, the priest. It is a terrible loss to give up one's father at such a tender age, but it was a great gain to be under the tutelage of Hilkiah and his fellow priests. Not only was I under that tutelage, but so were many members of my family, including Zephaniah, my cousin, whose devotion to the God of our fathers was evident early. He was a devoted student of the law and the prophets, and wise beyond his years. The Spirit of the Lord was in him. We grew close in those years of special schooling.

I, Josiah, wish this day to honor him, to tell you of the heritage he gave not only to me, but to you. It was he who helped me to understand the mysteries of Yahweh. He explained that Yahweh was a holy God who could not abide the corruption that tore apart our nation since the time of our grandfather, Manasseh. We spoke of it privately over and over. We were not alone, of course, but for three-quarters of a century no prophet dared to openly profane the names of the gods of our captors, the Assyrians. They were fearful. We were small; our enemies were big and powerful. Yet, our strength lay in Yahweh, whom we had not only ignored but dishonored by our idolatries. With the worship of Yahweh came the glue that held us together—the moral fiber of our nation. That glue was now gone. We were broken and demoralized. Zephaniah, however, was fearless. He had read the century-old prophecies of Amos and Isaiah. He echoed their predictions. Israel would suffer at the hands of her enemies until she learned. A day of wrath would come—a day of ruin and devastation. He condemned the leadership of the nation: politicians, priests, judges, and prophets. The Almighty would cleanse the people of their injustices. Likewise, Yahweh would judge the neighboring nations of Philistia, Moab, Cush, and even the mighty Assyria.

Because of Zephaniah's faith and his proclamation—his word from the Lord early in my adult reign—I sought the Lord with fervency about the state of our nation. The Lord gave me the courage to purge my nation of its idolatries and the attending leprosy of corruption. With this encouragement, I even reached out into the territories of the tribes of Israel, long alienated from us and even longer controlled by pagan Assyrians. In time, I saw the seed of disintegration in these pagan nations as prophesied by Amos, Isaiah, and my cousin Zephaniah. One of the nations that God used to cleanse them was the Scythians. They, in particular, hastened the demise of the Assyrian nation.

The carnage was only beginning,

> Sages say that when God says, through the prophet Zephaniah, "I shall bring dire distress on the people," God is referring to the distress that Moses would go through leading the people from captivity to freedom. When God spoke through the prophet, "they will walk like the blind," the reference is to the Israelites who would wander in the wilderness before another generation would be allowed to enter the promised land (*Exodus Rabbah* 42.4)

however. The purification of Yahweh's people was carried forth by another pagan nation, Babylon. "But joy is coming—joy is coming," said my cousin. "A remnant of our people will remain true, and the Lord who is king of Israel is with us. The Lord, mighty to save, will delight in his people. The Lord is King! The Lord reigns and will bring honor to this people throughout the earth."

"Zephaniah, you've given me hope. You've given us all courage for the future." *(Ed Thorn)*

Index of Readings
from *The Revised Common Lectionary*

Index
of Midrashim

Song of Songs Rabbah

Sefer Ha-Aggadah

Ginzberg